REAL ADVICE

for the

Newlywed

PLANNING YOUR LIFE TOGETHER

by Samuel Murphy

Real Advice for the Newlywed: Planning Your Life Together

by Samuel Murphy

COPYRIGHT © 2015

Photo Credits: Front cover photo of the funny couple ©Djem82. Author photo by Thomas Maher. Back cover photo of just married car ©Nacroba.

We are always happy to make corrections, include omissions or update information.

Email: books@relentlesslycreative.com
Phone: 773-831-4944.
Website: RelentlesslyCreativeBooks.com

ISBN- 978-1-942790-02-0

Relentlessly Creative Books

Dedication

FOR MY DAUGHTERS:
SHANNAN, DEVIN, MEGHAN, AND SIOBHAN

FOR THALIA, MY MUSE

Table of Contents

Foreword

by Mark Waters
Amazon's #1 Best Selling Author of
Three Days In Heaven

When Samuel asked me to write a foreword for his book *Real Advice for the Newlywed*, I did not hesitate. His first request was that I actually read it first and write an honest opinion. So this is me, being honest.

I am a busy writer with a busy life, and I tend to stay away from this sort of thing. My plan was simple, skim through the book and write a few nice things about it. Samuel even said himself that many men may not bother to read it (Same thing with men asking for directions.). Well, I did make time to read it, and my mind would not allow me to skim it. In fact, I could not put it down! I read every word, every line and every paragraph.

As an author myself, I am always interested in what makes stuff work, and as a kid, I would tear things apart to see what made them "tick." Unfortunately, I could not always put them back together.

REAL ADVICE

Sound familiar? Much like a marriage: sometimes easy to tear apart and harder (if not impossible) to put back together. Samuel's book not only teaches us how this marriage stuff works but also how to hold it together once we find it unraveling.

He has provided a "tool box" of knowledge and understanding in what makes us "tick" as humans. But more importantly, how to fix what we have broken. This book represents an owner's manual; one you can refer back to time and time again to resolve many problems that arise in your partnership, as well as preventing potential problems from happening in the first place.

Real Advice for the Newlywed, with its insightful approach, made me think and made me laugh. His deep and thorough knowledge on the subject is delivered in a tongue-in-cheek style that makes it an enjoyable and must read—by everyone.

I've been married to only one woman for nearly 38 years, and could fully relate to many of the issues he raised. I encourage anyone who is about to get married, recently married, or been at it for nearly a lifetime, read this book. I did and I loved it.

Introduction

"As humans, we spend most of our lives holding our breath...until we find that special someone who simply takes it away."

This is a book about choices. Life is full of them. Depending on who you ask, and whether you throw every decision you make into the mix, we average between 600 and 35,000 choices each and every day. The fact is, some folks estimate that we will make almost 8 million choices in our lifetime. One group from Cornell cited that we make over 225 decisions each day about food alone. Of course, everyone is giving numbers based on the average person. Obviously, if you are doing time in Folsom Prison, you're making about 2 decisions a day, and curiously, one of them was to select this book from the prison library.

According to my calculations, if you take the average lifespan in general for both sexes; subtract the first fifteen years of life, when nobody lets you have any choices, then take away all the Sundays when your only thought is how you are going to face another Monday; add back in your half-witted Friday Happy Hour decisions when your judgment may be rather impaired (and thus become statistical outliers); then divide it all by my secret formula, you get between 300 to 400 decisions per day.

REAL ADVICE

Sounds about right.

But whether it's 60 or 600, some choices are rather trivial in the Grand Scheme of things: soft taco shells or crunchy? Vera Wang Scarf with Giorgio Armani? Provolone or Cheez Whiz?

Other choices we make each day carry a bit more heft: What college should I attend? Should I take this job? Is it time to go out on my own? If I'm careful, can I light the barbecue with some gasoline?

Should I marry this guy? Should I marry this girl?

Ah, and here we are, right at the heart of the matter, just five paragraphs in.

There are other extremely important choices you will make in the fullness of time, but this one...this one concerning whom you will spend the rest of your life with, trumps everything on the board. It's the Big Enchilada. The Big Bopper. The Big Bang. (Not the TV show; the Stephen Hawking/Carl Sagan thing.)

Virtually every decision you make for the rest of your life will be somehow inextricably linked to this one choice. But remember this: All choices have consequences; and as the Grail Knight in "Indiana Jones and the Last Crusade" said, "Choose wisely."

For the females reading this, I am well aware that you are pretty much in charge of all this wedding business stuff. Even though your man got down on one knee and did his best to sound like a really cool adult as he proposed, chances are he was pretty much absolved of all responsibility for the actual planning and completion of the wedding arrangements. As a visual aid, just think back to all

4

those nature films you have seen where the male lion is instrumental in the procreation business. He then figures his job is done and mom will take care of the rest. He sleeps, he eats (food provided by the lioness), and he rolls over on his belly. In short, he's pretty much useless after all that sex stuff.

As for you men reading this, you will definitely see yourself (maybe that lion analogy self). Usually, it's not very pretty, but that's OK. There are a lot of things you are responsible for and I will do my best to help you face married life like a man and not lose any of your masculinity, pride or dignity.

I promise I will poke fun at both sexes. In between, I will do my best to offer some real, solid, and quite serious advice to you concerning married life in all of its forms; from housing, to financial planning, disagreements, division of labor, children, pets, in-laws, and the rest of the gamut that represents pre and post marital life. My aim is to give you advice that will not only help you survive in it, but thrive in it. After all, every marriage (like that bottle of hot sauce you have in your refrigerator) should last a lifetime.

Just please keep in mind that some (most) human actions and reactions to stress, mistakes, challenges, and the like are indeed funny and many will be pointed out.

Of course, since this is a book filled with a lot of "How To's," it will probably not see many readers who happen to be men. After all, when was the last time the man pulled off the road to look at the Rand McNally, or read the directions on how to install that flat screen TV that had to be returned two hours after it was purchased with the telltale scorch marks that were, "Just there when I took it out of the box?"

REAL ADVICE

What I'm trying to say here is that, as a professional, I will do whatever I can to tell the unabashed story, truthfully explain the intricacies, and shed some serious light on what newlywed life can be from an evenhanded point of view. In short, I won't gloss over anything.

There are so many books on marriage and how to handle your newfound fame, along with all the obligatory blogs, seminars, and advice columns that try to help you in your wedding planning and married life. And yes, they do serve a purpose. They really do. But let's be honest. Many of them truly gloss over (or just don't deal with) the real, honest to God, down in the dirt human actions, reactions and emotions that don't always solve problems the way any of us would hope. Especially from people, who on many occasions aren't thinking so clearly. Usually, their advice ends up with: "Make a list..." "Sit down with your mate and..." "Be honest about..." "Never..." "Always..." "Have a frank exchange..." "Marriage counseling can be a great..."

The fact is, most of us are not list makers, sit downers to share, frankly exchangers, neverers, carers and sharers, alwaysers or bearers of our souls to someone who we don't know. Most of us are, "ChristAlmighty, what a crappy day I've had, and I'd make a list of it all but I can't find that damn pencil in the junk drawer, and I REALLY don't want to talk or share ANYTHING with you until I've had some wine, and for Godssake, if you leave your filthy underwear on the floor just one more time... I hate you." kind of people.

Marriage, even the one that is new, isn't always hearts and flowers. It can be just as messy as that junk drawer you can't find a list-making pencil in.

So, what will we be doing here? Well, not only will we take a look at past events in your life and a look into your current situation (I'm guessing that you are checking out this book because either your nuptials are imminent, or the thing has recently been done), but more importantly, we will be looking into the future—helping you deal with problems before they start.

In short, we will see what brought you here, how to handle stuff now that you have arrived, and most importantly, take a look at future events and how you will deal with them as well as how you should deal with them.

Together, you and I are going to focus on the real human touch of interactions and the oft-times chaotic and sloppy surroundings that so often besets people who are simply trying their damnedest to make a go of it, and how much all of it can interfere with their day-to-day wellbeing. Amid all of this clutter and disarray, is where most of the human population lives.

As you read, just keep in mind that you are human, and as such, you will do human things. And there will be times when you just simply can't take it any more and do something stupid. Or you may actually do something that you promised yourself you would never ever do. There will be times when you will worry about falling short, to yourself, and your mate. There will be times when you truly do fall short. And of course, you will experience times when your mate falls completely short.

You also need to know that you have the ability to fix it all before it gets the better of you. And that's what we're going to concentrate on.

OK, so much for the Introduction. Now for the show.

CHAPTER ONE

What The Hell Just Happened?

The inevitable has finally happened, hasn't it? You got married. Tied the knot. Joined in connubial bliss. Bit the bullet. Took yourself out of circulation. Just became celibate. Made the biggest mistake of your life. Made the smartest decision you have ever made in your life.

Congratulations.

You are now paired along with about 2.3 million other couples who will get married this year in the United States alone. That's about 6,300 marriages each and every day. Going on down the line, that works out to approximately 260 marriages each hour. I divided by 24 because you need to remember that the Vegas wedding chapels offer 24 hour a day service, 7 days a week. I think they have drive up windows and everything.

Some more fun facts that might interest you include the numbers 25 and 28. That's the average age of the bride and groom, respectively. One-third of those getting married have been married before. The average number of guests invited to a wedding is around 178. We Americans spend about $72 billion on weddings each year. Yes, billion. The average wedding budget is around $20,000, including that idiot DJ who never gets the songs right. A tad over $1,000 is the cost of wedding rings for both the bride and the groom. The average honeymoon budget is almost $4,000.

And in this economy.

My Advice? The average funeral costs $6,000. So, my first piece of advice is to get going on that honeymoon, then die because of the cost differences.

Now, for all of you who are reading this, go back and compare the above short list of wedding facts to what you recently went through. Don't worry whether the numbers I ticked off are true or not, just accept the fact that they look official. We don't need to stand around so you can question their veracity.

Did your experience measure up? Were you close in your budgeting? Did you get that $1,000 ring? The $4,000 honeymoon? Were you exhaustipated after greeting and thanking all 178 guests who showed up? Any money left from that twenty grand? Were you constantly yelling at the DJ throughout the evening because he wouldn't play "Stairway to Heaven," but played "The Chicken Dance" on a loop?

If, after an honest assessment you find that somehow you got short changed, there is one more statistic you may want to know: Out of all the marriages in the United States this year, over 800,000 will end in divorce before that first year anniversary rolls around. Actually, if you work it out mathematically (and who doesn't just love to do that), overall there is a divorce in the U.S. every 1 ½ minutes each day. That's about 2,200 per day!

Busy, busy, busy.

So take a look around. If you don't see a fine, sparkly rock on your left hand, or you remember eating egg salad sandwiches and drinking flat, warmish beer at the reception, or your house is not filled to the brim with all those cool gifts your 178 guests bought you, and the only pictures you have from your honeymoon are those stupid phone camera selfies of you and your spouse playing miniature golf at Six Flags, I have some other euphemisms for you:

You're in between marriages right now. You're doing some matrimonial restructuring. The position of husband/wife has been eliminated. You've been relieved of your marital duties and all things matrimonial. Your current status of husband/wife has been outsourced. Your marriage has gone to live on a farm with a very nice family in Vermont.

Well, maybe you better wait on this part. After all, you are just getting married, and if you move too quickly on that above stuff, you're gonna have to give back all those nice wedding gifts you received. No more fake crystal wine glasses, or Wal-Mart blenders, or place mats with palm tree designs on them, or silver plated Ronco shrimp forks.

"Shrimp forks? Who in the hell gave us shrimp forks?"

But not the money. You don't have to give back the money. I don't know if Miss Manners said that or what, but you don't have to give back the cash. Besides, the last bit of dough taken from one of those envelopes you received at the reception was spent on that round of putt-putt golf at Six Flags.

Regardless of whether you found yourself in paragraph four, or checked all of the "no" boxes in paragraph eleven, here you are. Bound in wedded bliss with your soul mate forever and ever. For better or worse.

My Advice? Whether your marriage was as humble as the pie you're going to have to eat for the next 60 years or so, or as gilded as a Kardashian hemline, should you ever be having a very heated argument, please don't ever remind your spouse about them sandwiches and warmish beer. You will regret this. Besides, the kind of wedding you have just had, or will soon have, will ultimately always lose out to the fact that you got through it, and did it for all of the right reasons.

We now land in today. No matter what has come before, you may have woken up this morning as one half of a married couple. All the fuss and the planning and the alterations and the running around are over. No more of the 287 back and forth phone calls each day, each one asking the same thing: "Honey, what do you think about...?" In fact, no more questions at all that are answered, "Whatever," "I really don't care anymore. Just do it," and, "I'm sorry, Dave is not here at the moment. Please leave your name and number at the beep." No more chaos. No more, "I know we can't afford it, but it will make him/her so happy." No more, "GoddamnJesusHChrist, I can't wait for this to be all over!"

Whew.

Well, it is finally over and you are just back from your honeymoon. Everything is a bit more settled. The guests have all gone. The well wishers and family have departed. The DJ got caught up in a drug sweep and won't be doing any weddings for quite some time. The wedding gifts have all been lovingly put in their proper places. You have moved the rest of your belongings into your new home. All is as it should be. Any questionable memories and silly arguments that came before have been put aside or simply forgotten. You are finally able to take a deep breath, make yourself a nice refreshing drink using that new Wal-Mart blender (before the thing burns itself out and throws up all over your nice kitchen wallpaper due to shoddy workmanship performed somewhere deep in the bowels of China), and settle comfortably and securely into your new life.

It's now evening. Dinner is finished. The table has been cleared. You sit in your cozy chair, perhaps with a cat on your lap, reading this book. Dim lighting casts soft shadows on the walls that playfully dance around you. You are enveloped in silence and peace. All is quiet. All is as it should be.

Looking up from your book, you survey the room and gently and lovingly stroke your cat's velvety fur, thinking how lucky you are. The house is perfect. The person you married is perfect. Your life together is perfect. The book you are reading is perfect. The cat is perfect.

Yet in the quiet stillness of your reverie, there's something. Something in the back... Something dark. Something slightly off. Shapeless, but there. Somewhere in the back... Your stomach tightens. You can feel your face becoming flushed and warm. There is a slight copper taste in your mouth from the adrenaline rush now coursing through your body. In the quietness of your room, you can hear your own heart beating. Getting closer now. Becoming more visible, but still difficult to make out. Oh my God. There it is. It can't be! Please say it's not what I think it is! Oh God! Oh God! Oh God!

Oh shit!

REAL ADVICE

Why, it's Self Doubt. In retail sales it's called Buyer's Remorse.

Who in the hell let you in?

Self doubt or buyer's remorse go by many other names and quite possibly you would prefer something a bit softer such as, "Now that all the hubbub and festivities are over, (or they're just about to commence) it's time to get serious and start making some real honest to God plans so we don't get left behind, and, as author Chinua Achebe would say, "Things Fall Apart."

That may be a better description, but it's way too long and hard to write. So we'll stick with whatever nametag works.

Suddenly, for the first time (at least since the wedding rehearsal) you may still have a question or two. Questions like, "What did I just do?" "Who is this person next to me?" (Not the cat. The other one, the one on two legs). "What was I thinking?" "What do I do now?"

All good questions, but don't keep it up. Because it will all end in a very bad place, with you asking more questions like, "Am I really going to get to hang out with my friends?" Is he/she going to go ballistic when I burn the mashed potatoes?" "How am I going to balance home, work, family, finish this book, pet this cat, and handle my marriage all at the same time?" "How much time needs to pass before I feel comfortable farting in front of him?" "How's she gonna like me now that she sees just how nasty my underwear can get?" "Well, let's find out."

"Where did I put the shovel?"

You may have asked yourself these questions once before; probably during the time you were contemplating marriage and trying your best to answer that, "Honey, what do you think about...?" question during the wedding planning. But at that point, the "I do's" were far enough away and you would worry about it all later. Because right now there are bachelor parties to be planned. Bridal showers to attend, a DJ to hire. Lots and lots of shopping to do. Lots of opportunities to toast with lots and lots of alcohol. Announcements to get out. Wedding dresses. Food tastings. Cheap, ill fitting tuxedos. Seating arrangements so that every single shirttail relative and friend would be satisfied with their placement. And the cake. Mmmm, cake. Bride's Maids to be chosen. Lots and lots of crying over (as well as special alterations to) those damned glow in the dark, lime-green bridesmaids dresses. Groomsmen to pick (the ones who could bring the beer bongs). Cute kids to do the flower throwing thing and the ring-bearing thing. Maybe some more alcohol. That one last little fling with... well, you get the idea.

But now it's all come home to you. You're married. At the first sign of trouble, you can't (at least not legally) grab the hammer, give your new spouse a couple of whacks, wrap him or her up in a shower curtain, call Uncle Guido and tell him to get some lye and come pick up the "package." (Making sure you find that shovel before he gets there.)

You can't take him/her back to the store. You have no receipt, and he/she was marked "as is" anyway. No returns. And finally, you can't pretend it never happened. You can't say it must have been the rohypnol or the scotch or the crazy Gypsy Cat Lady down the street who gave you the "evil eye." Besides, you probably left a pretty long legal paper trail that would be easy to trace back to you.

Maybe it is time for you to reminisce a bit, and access those regions of your brain that aren't in emotional overdrive right now and try to honestly remember what it was that got you here in the first place.

You know, that list of things that attracted you to your soul mate.

Maybe it was those baby blues. The ones you lost yourself in. Maybe it was his/her easy-going nature. The kindness she possessed. The consideration he always showed to you. The patience each one of you had for each other. The compassion you both felt for one another. The way she pulled on her hair when she was nervous or embarrassed. The way his hair fell around his forehead in that little boy haphazard way. Her nose. His chin. Her legs. His hands. The ability to make each other laugh. The completeness you felt when you were around one another.

Or maybe, and possibly closer to the truth, it's was her breasts. His butt. The alcohol. The pheromones. Her tiny waist. His tiny waist. (Check back with me on that one in about ten years.) The desire and the desperation not to go through another Friday night all by yourself. The bet you made with your idiot friends about how you could "tap" that. The bet you made with your friends about how you could "tame" that. The heat. The sweat. The hot, passion of a summer's eve.

No doubt, it was a combination of the above and hundreds of additional reasons, some so subtle that even now you can't exactly put your finger on them, but you know they are there. All these things helped dictate your decision before you got down on your knees and asked for her hand in marriage; or you stood there while he was on his knees and said, "Yes, I'll marry you."

You may think that how you got here isn't really that important. It may not seem that way now, but trust me, it is. How you got on that merry-go-round that ended up with you sitting in your cozy little chair, reading this book, and stroking that cat, says and means a lot.

Author's Note: Now before we go any further, let me assure you, or reassure you, that I am fully aware not all couples go through this buyer's remorse thing (or that really long titled thing) individually or collectively. Some do, some don't. For those who do, the intensity and manifestations vary widely. Add to that, men will go through this much differently than women. Psychologically speaking, it's all very complex, and it will give you quite a migraine before too long. If you find yourself experiencing this, not to worry. It's normal. It will pass. You will be fine.

Here's How it All Works:

We are all products of both our environment and nature. Please tell me you remember at least that part of high school biology. You know: nature/nurture. It's not just nature. It's not just nurture. Both shape us. Each one plays an incredibly important role and explains how we act, react, and live our lives. In my incredibly long and superficial way, allow me to explain.

First, The Chemical Part:

Human beings have literally hundreds if not thousands of opportunities to interact with other human beings each and every day. Whether it's through personal contact or electronic, virtually everyone on the planet is (or can be in an instant) connected to each other in one way or another.

REAL ADVICE

You can start up and maintain a relationship with someone in Senegal or Bahrain. You can do business quite easily with someone whose corporate headquarters is located in Indonesia. You can LinkedIn, Instagram, Tumble, Tweet, Facebook, Blog, Pinit, Reddit, StumbleUpon, blah, blah, blah to millions of others just by pressing a button or two.

Remarkable when you think about it.

But most of our real, lasting relationships take place much, much closer to home: the grocery store, our workplace, our church, our college campus, or the local bar. These are those fascinating face-to-face encounters that provide us with lasting friendships as well as eternal loves. So I'm betting that most of you met your future mate somewhere close to your own turf (meeting at college doesn't count, because even though both of you may be far from home, you're in close proximity at the college you're attending).

If you did happen to find your mate in Bahrain or Senegal, well, GoodGodDamn for you.

Just remember this: These encounters with each other are not as haphazard and accidental as you might think. This is because in the Grand Design of the universe, things are not without a plan.

For instance, it has been noted that women look for certain types of men during certain cyclical episodes occurring in their lives (the estrogen thing). During ovulation, a woman is more apt to be attracted to virility in a man rather than any other characteristic. She is likely to desire being close to those men who exude (literally) all the physical traits that, well, make a man a man. In short, she may seek a really good procreator, someone who promotes the survival of the species in a "survival of the strongest" kind of way. Strong, physical male + strong genes = hardy offspring who will be strong enough to survive in case World War Z ever really comes to pass (at least longer than the movie did).

Now during her menstruation (yes, I said it), she is more apt to be attracted to a man who exudes more intellectual characteristics: A man who is likely to be well grounded with a good sense of humor, and who would be a good provider. He can look as virile as the above example, but that is not the characteristic she is looking for. She's looking for steady, long lasting bonding. No straying Tomcats.

By the way, even though a woman can be attracted to a more sensitive man during menstruation who may look virile, she is more than likely to be attracted to men that possess more oval, feminine shaped faces. Interesting as hell, isn't it?

This is all due to complex brain and body chemistry and pheromones doing whatever loop-de-loops during whatever time of the month it is. We are specifically dealing with the chemistry of mating here. There is much more at play, (the nurture part) but let's not get ahead of ourselves.

Author's Note: The above information about what type of man a woman might be attracted to is not meant to be sexist or sexually biased, or in any way meant to degrade or scar anyone's sensibilities. It's just some scientific stuff based on real studies by real doctors in real labs with vials and beakers and foaming solutions. Some of this information comes from the United States of America's Government. Some comes from some studies at Duke (I think) and the University of Colorado (I think). I probably should include some footnotes in here somewhere, but it would feel like we were all back in college, and you and I both know, this book will not be included in the syllabus. Trust me on this, or Google it and see for yourself.

And it's all true. Swear to God.

Now, testosterone laden, single men, drunk or sober, and lacking a marker or two in their DNA chain, just look for one thing, and have only one question: "What woman in her right mind would come home with me tonight? She really doesn't have to be in her right mind, or have one at all for that matter."

Again, I'm not ragging on the male stereotype here. What a male's hormones are telling him is essentially the same thing a woman's hormones are telling her at one time or another: Produce more offspring. Strong offspring. Offspring who are strong enough to survive, and in turn, do their part in providing more offspring themselves so as to continue carrying on the human species.

In short, the children really are our future.

Unlike a woman however, men's cycles don't have much of a clear transitional stage. Outwardly, men seem like the same, "Lookwhativegotforyou" kind of guy 24 hours a day. But trust me, on the inside he really does go through his cycles. His cycles, however, are more predicated on her cycles. The closer a woman gets to ovulation, the more his eyes light up like a pinball machine. Again, it's the pheromone thing. Like a shark, he can literally smell it. And it's mostly in her armpits.

All this is called the "Biological Imperative," and many scientists swear by it. It not only affects our thinking about sexual reproduction, but other human characteristics as well, such as bonding, altruism, monogamy, competitiveness, territoriality, sexual orientation, and so on. These are things in your life that you don't actually choose, but you think you do.

And it's not just the estrogen/testosterone chemical reactions that are motivating you to be attracted to someone. There's a lot more at play.

Without getting way too scientific here, there are many other hormones that dictate your attraction and bonding to your prospective mate. Among the big three are serotonin, dopamine and norepinephrine.

About 80% of your serotonin lives in your digestive system, and yes, that's where that, "I just felt something in my gut." statement comes from. It aids not only in digestion, but sexual desire as well. The other 20% lives in your brain and it is that hormone that helps with calmness and serenity.

Interestingly, some researchers at a university in the UK found that people in love had about the same low levels of serotonin as people with OCD. This explains why one or both partners can't stop thinking about each other (That's not a joke: they actually said that.).

Dopamine is another hormone that plays a huge role in attraction. Dopamine helps us with such things as elation, energy, cravings, motivation and obsession. All in all, it's a busy little hormone, isn't it?

It's also produced in the brain, and it shoots out into other brain areas very, very quickly. So quickly in fact that this is where the, "It was love at first sight," statement comes from.

The last of the big three is norepinephrine. This hormone is very close to adrenaline, and we all know what that hormone is all about. And like adrenaline it can increase your blood pressure as well as your blood glucose levels (sugar). So I would presume that's where the terms like "Sugar Pie," "Sweetie," "Honey Pie" and all the rest of those sophomoric platitudes come from.

I'm really taking a chance of losing you here, but I need to just briefly touch on two more hormones: oxytocin and vasopressin.

Don't roll your eyes. This stuff is important because it's sex stuff.

Both men and women release these hormones after sex and they help deepen the bond between two people. So, many of the scientists firmly believe that the more sex, the greater the bond. In fact, the hormone oxytocin is often referred to as, "The Cuddle Hormone." Isn't that sweet?

Vasopressin is another important hormone in the long-term commitment stage and is released after sex.

Vasopressin works with your kidneys to control thirst. Its potential role in long-term relationships was "accidently" discovered when scientists looked at the prairie vole. A vole is a small rodent. Think mouse with a stouter body. A prairie vole is a vole that lives in our Great Western Plains.

Getting all of this?

Anyway, prairie voles indulge in far more sex than is strictly necessary for the purposes of reproduction. Like humans, they form fairly stable pair-bonds.

When male prairie voles were given a drug that suppressed the effect of vasopressin, the bond with their partner deteriorated immediately as they lost their devotion and failed to protect their partner from new suitors.

Author's Note: Please forgive me if you think I'm reducing every human emotion to a bunch of chemical actions and reactions taking place in your body. I'm not, but in the main, that's the long and short of it. And while you may think that this takes all the poetry out of love and relationships, it really doesn't. Besides, in finding a mate and partner with whom we passionately desire to spend the rest of our lives with, who wants to rely solely on the transient nature of chemicals and chemical reactions?

Believe me, it is those same chemical actions and reactions that blow the top of your head off when you meet the love of your life. Those chemicals that brought your glands together are the same ones that melt your heart, and make you weak in the knees. They are the same ones that give you that zingy feeling in the pit of your stomach (And you know... the other place.). And incidentally, especially for you men: It is those chemicals that, when opening your mouth to this beautiful example of womanhood for the first time, you are so hyped with infatuation and chemically created emotions that all you manage to get out is "Hummina, hummina, hummina." This is why so many women think all men are idiots.

Thanks, man.

No. Love and other emotions are real and become so much more as they snap and fire off in your head and heart as to transcend many of those biological imperatives. Besides, believing too much in the chemistry puts way too much stock in nature and not enough in nurture.

REAL ADVICE

Let's just put it simply and leave it all behind us: Everything bad about your genetic makeup and your physical features came from your father's side of the family. Everything good about your genetic makeup and physical features came from your mother's side of the family. I don't make this up as I go along. Trust it to be true and move on.

Now To The Nurture Part:

The experiences we have gone through in our lives also heavily shape us in how we view the world and how we react to it: When you didn't get picked for the team. When someone said you couldn't accomplish something. When someone called you a name. Not having clothes in the same style as your friends. Not having friends. Dad was always on you. Mom would not let you grow up. No prom date. No pets.

On the flip side, perhaps your mom and dad were perfect and completely supportive of virtually everything you did. Lots of friends. An overload of prospects with whom to attend the prom. Reasonable success in academics and sports. Nice clothes. Well liked by all. Nice house. A weekly allowance. A cute little puppy.

Good, bad or indifferent, the life you went through leading up to this moment has been heavily influenced by the things you went through weeks, months, and years ago. In a large part you are who you are because of it. And it's these memories of your life—not your DNA—that either keep you awake at night or help you to sleep.

It's also these experiences that help, in their own little ways, in giving you this self doubt I spoke of earlier: "I hope I'm not going to be like my father." "I hope I will be just as wonderful a wife as my mom has been to my dad." "Man, don't let me mess this thing up." "What if I can't..." "What if she..." What if he..." What if I..."

What does all of this nurture stuff mean? It means that we filter many of our actions and reactions through the previous experiences we have gone through in our lives, and how we interact with cats, dogs, people, the clerk at the grocery store and livestock, is predicated on those experiences.

Always remember: your emotions are yours and yours alone. But so often we are prone to say things like, "You make me so..." and "I did that because you..."

Nobody can really make you feel a certain way. Your reaction to happiness, sadness, good news, bad news, life challenges and ultimately falling in love is because of your past experiences, whether good or bad.

That's nurture.

Now whether you come down more heavily on the chemistry than on the heart, or vice versa, this self doubt/post wedding blues/buyer's remorse thing you may be going through is caused more by the nurture part of you than the chemical part of you. After all, you're dealing with human expectations, emotions, and your own past experiences here, as well as living up to the enormous societal and familial pressure in general to succeed. Remember, you've probably witnessed marriages or close relationships either fall apart or thrive in your lifetime, and maybe on some level you felt the effects from it. THAT'S an experience. THAT's nurture. Fair or not, there are high demands on you from all quarters.

That's a lot of pressure.

REAL ADVICE

Incidentally, regardless of the chemistry (nature) part that played a large role in you two getting together, many times (not always, as we are not dealing with absolutes here) the nurture part is why many men marry their mothers and why many women marry their fathers. It is also why many men marry the antithesis of their mothers, and why many women marry the antithesis of their fathers. This is largely because of an individual's growing up years (nurture).

If you think about it, it makes perfect sense. Dad is tall and lean. Husband is tall and lean. Mom is blonde and blue eyed. Wife is blonde and blue eyed. Dad could fix just about anything. Husband is very handy with his hands. Mom could bake. Wife is a great baker.

On the antithesis side, dad is short and rather heavy. Husband is tall and lean. Mom is raven haired with intense dark eyes. Wife is blonde and blue eyed. Dad couldn't change a tire. Husband is an auto mechanic. Mom boiled everything. Wife can really bake.

Close to home, my daughter number two just got married. The man she wed is tall and lean. I am not. He has dark hair. I do not. His eyes are dark. Mine are not. He is extremely intelligent. As you can probably tell, I am an idiot. This is the antithesist child.

On the other hand, daughter number four is currently dating a young man who looks suspiciously like I did at his age (except his hair is much longer. GoodGodAlmighty.). Daughter number three refuses to date anyone while she concentrates on her music career. Daughter number one is currently involved with a young man who has many of my attributes but with dark hair. He is not, however, an idiot.

So it's a mixed bag in my family. Me? Well, I married a woman who in many ways is nothing like my mother, but who mothers me quite well. She's a nurse by trade and safeguards me from many potential eating misadventures and personal injuries. My wife married a man (me) who in many ways is like her father. He passed away before we were married, but I hear he was an idiot too.

Regardless of which scenario you find yourself in marriage wise, you can't hold only nature responsible for it. It's the life you grew up in. And those experiences helped shape your choices in a very large way.

So it's nature/nurture. The first, nature, is virtually impossible to alter. The other, nurture, is really up to the individual to transcend.

But now, back to the real to-do. During these moments of self-examinations, what kind of person are you really? Let's take a look at the following—

CHAPTER TWO

Who The Hell Am I?

Who The Hell Are You?

So here you are, possibly going through some form of post-wedding depression, wondering what comes next. The marathon of your marriage has only just begun. If you listen, you can still hear the echo of the starter's pistol ringing in your ears and you are both barely across the starting line. You have another twenty, thirty, forty, fifty, or more years left until you get to Heartbreak Hill and cross the finish line. And that's a long time to keep everything together.

So even though you may be doubting your own capabilities and qualifications; un-cup your hands and let those thoughts fly away (It's a very Zen thing to do. It doesn't hurt for you to be a little trendy.). Chances are you married right. The person you are now sharing everything with, was, and still is, and shall forever be one of the best decisions you have ever made. Each of you is completely content with the other. You are both deeply in love with one another, and maybe for the first time in your life you have found your own personal heaven. Stop looking at any of the negatives whether they exist in your life or in your mate's. Let me wave my hand in front of your face and say very slowly, "These aren't the droids you're looking for."

I hope I have made that clear.

This self-doubt you may have (I say "may have" because remember, not every married individual goes through this) leads to self-examination. And what human being doesn't just love to sit around and be brutally honest about who he or she really, truly is? After all, we all signed up for Facebook, and we can go on it daily to reaffirm how cool and wonderful our "friends" find us.

But self-examination, and I mean real self-examination can be quite a liberating process. Among other things, it can help you come to terms with your "self," and help identify what kind of person you truly are.

As a case in point, let's take a quick look at one incident from a long time ago.

In an interview many years ago, the famous interviewer, Barbara Walters asked the famous actress, Katharine Hepburn, "If you were a tree, what kind of tree would you be?"

Just like "Plan 9 From Outer Space," was for years considered the worst movie of all time, (supplanted recently by "Batman and Robin") this question was considered the dumbest interview question of all time (recently supplanted by, "Can your baby get pregnant if you have sex while you're pregnant?").

Well because of that, (or maybe in spite of that) the tree question is the one we're going to focus on to help further explain the nurture part of our lives. So, what are you? Are you like the oak tree: Unbending. Strong. Resilient. Able to stand firmly in place while strong winds swirl around you. Are you like the willow: Soft. Pliable. Able to bend while strong winds swirl about. Perhaps you are a bit of both.

Perhaps you are a perfect example of the Baobab tree.

For those of you who have never heard of this tree, the African Baobab is sometimes called the Tree of Life. However, this is not for spiritual or theological reasons. The tree is so useful, that it is able to help sustain life in many ways. Baobabs provide food, a fruit called "Monkey Bread." This fruit provides people with a sustainable source of vitamin C. Scientists think that the Baobab tree could be a potential answer to major world health problems. Baobab bark is used to make rope and cloth, and to use as tools or clothing. In addition to all these uses, Baobab trunks also serve as shelter. Isn't that nice? Sort of like "The Giving Tree."

Maybe you are more like the Albino Redwood Tree. The Albino Redwood is sort of like a plant vampire. It sucks its nutrients from other redwood trees by burrowing into their roots.

The really amazing thing is, not just do they suck the nutrients from their parent tree (they can reproduce asexually as shoots from roots) but also, they can do it for up to a 100 years. The only reason that albino redwoods survive at all is that they are connected at the root to the other tree from which they will suck energy for their entire lives.

REAL ADVICE

Yikes.

You getting any of this?

Of course, you're not locked into only the above suggestions. Maybe you consider yourself a Wisteria. This is a tree that just stands around looking really, really pretty.

By the way, in response to that question from Barbara Walters, Ms. Hepburn declared that if she had to be a tree, she would prefer to be an oak.

Me? Personally, I would be a Maple Tree. Mmmmm... ..pancakes.

Okay, enough about trees before this thing turns into a coffee table book with full color photos of flora from around the world.

But let's face it; you're like at least one of them. Are you strong and unbending? Are you strong because you're yielding? Are you a giver of life? Are you a taker? Are you just pretty?

Nothing wrong with being pretty, by the way.

Of course, dealing with long-term consequences, the mighty, unbending oak, although it has a very deep root system, can get broken in two by a very strong wind. The willow, as you probably know, will bend in whichever direction the wind blows. The wisteria? Well, again, there's nothing wrong in just standing around looking pretty.

My Advice? Be very careful with which one you identify with. Every characteristic of every type of character has its positive and negative energy.

And who you are, how you react to all those marital moments you will face from this day forward (or shortly) possibly can dictate just how happy you will be and just how long things will last. As I said, you're just starting. And as much as you know about him/her, there is so much inside the other person that still remains a mystery.

So what do you have to look forward to? For many of you reading this, there are going to be a whole bunch of firsts. And that's partly what this book is about: To expose you to the firsts and how to handle all of them before they handle you. (By the way, if you've been living with your now new spouse for like ten years before you finally got married, you've already covered some of this ground, but don't worry, there are hidden traps aplenty for you. So please just be patient while I talk to the newbies.

So what do we mean by firsts?

It doesn't matter how long you knew each other before you married, and how well synched you may think you are: Did you know he likes Salisbury Steak and beer from a bottle, not a can. That he also likes floral prints and hot chocolate by the buckets. Does he know that you really hate Salisbury Steak, and you'll take beer in a can, but you really wish someone would offer you a nice Chardonnay once in awhile. Does he know you can take the floral prints, but only in the summer, and there really is only so much hot chocolate a person can take? For him, "Is that more wine she's drinking? Is her ass growing? She better not start looking like her mother." For her, "Is that another one of his hairs in the sink? He needs to eat a little less carbs." "He better not start smelling like his father."

There are still lots and lots to go over. Still lots of things to find out about.

REAL ADVICE

You will have your first discussion over finances as a married couple. You will have your first fight over finances as a married couple. You will have your first discussion as a married couple about where the couch goes. You will have your first fight as a married couple about where the couch goes. You will have your first discussion as a married couple about how he likes his clean socks matched and folded fresh from the dryer and neatly put in the second drawer of his side of the dresser. (That's because his mother used to do the laundry for him). You will have your first fight as a married couple about that he is not broken and he can put his own Goddamn socks away himself.

There will be the first discussion as a married couple about the toilet seat. Up? Down? Take the whole thing off? There will be the first fight as a married couple about him ignoring the whole toilet seat issue and just peeing off the back porch like some six year old. Chicken for dinner? With peas. Always with peas. The History Channel or Lifetime tonight? Should we also have a TV in the bedroom? "You're going to wear that?" "Are you ready yet?" "Which car do you want to take?" "Your birthday is the fifth, right? Or is our anniversary the fifth, and your birthday is on the tenth?"

"Where the hell is that shovel?" "I hate you."

And there are so many more joint discussions and decisions. Your parent's house for Thanksgiving? My parent's house for Christmas? Joint savings, but separate checking? Dog or cat? Both? "Have you fed the dog?" "Have you fed the cat?" "Honey, what's your Yahoo account password?" "I saw your old girlfriend, Lisa, at the grocery store today. Boy, she's put on some weight. What did you see in her anyway?" "Saw your old boyfriend at the bar last night. I think he's gay now. What did you see in him anyway?"

And on and on and on.

Now obviously, you and your new spouse will not spend every waking moment concerning monumental decisions and crossing swords over every situation you will both encounter. And God forbid you spend most of your time fighting about anything at all.

But these little things are traps, and you can get caught up in them easier than you think. Personally, I think all marriages would work out if it wasn't for the day-to-day mechanics of living so close to each other. This nearness, by the way, is what social psychologists call "propinquity."

And most marriages do work out. After all, the divorce rate is around 40%, which means, of course, that about 60% of marriages succeed. This isn't a huge margin, but it is encouraging.

Besides, in between all of these discussions, decisions, and yes, altercations, there's a lot of shared joy, blissful days and dreamy nights. Steamy passion, everlasting memories, utter contentment, and unabashed, simple down in the dirt, up in the clouds, everyday, everlasting love. All of this might read like a country song, but that's a lot of good stuff.

Of course, we haven't gotten to the sex part or the "What about children?" part, or the, "Your cousin's going to stay how long? " part, or the, "Is that what you really think of my mother?" part or the, "Is that what you really think of me?" part. "...I hate you."

My Advice? Now that you're married, you're going to be faced with obstacles, problems, decisions, and choices that

REAL ADVICE

you and your spouse will need to deal with like real adults. Facing them together and working through them together is the key. And along the way, you just may find out what kind of tree you really are.

And please, please, please... you may just view this as an unoriginal aphorism, but try to keep in mind that the best person to talk to about the problems in your relationship is the person you are in the relationship with.

So let's go to what happens next and take a look at what all the fuss was about in the first place.

CHAPTER THREE

What Do We Do Now?

A long time ago, there was a movie called, "The Candidate." By a long time ago, I mean it was made in 1972. (That's last century if you're keeping track. I know I am.) It starred a very young Robert Redford who looked and acted the part of the quintessential robustly handsome, very hip politician. Like the kind of guy women are attracted to whether they are ovulating or not. (Please pretend I inserted the disclaimer from Chapter One here, and let's move on. Don't want to get bogged down in legalese.)

Anyway, he was running a campaign to become the Junior Senator from the State of California, and went through minefield after minefield to reach his goal. Back then, the movie was known for its honest portrayal of all the crap a candidate for public office needed to go through to get elected.

So here we are at the end of the movie, election won, supporters gathered, acceptance speech written. In the back of the hotel where the candidate was trying to make his way onto the stage to thank the throng of wildly enthusiastic loyalists, and completely smothered in reporters who machine gunned questions at him, he (Redford) taps his campaign manager on the shoulder and drags him into a small utility room off the hotel's kitchen.

The campaign manager (played by Peter Boyle) enters the room and there's Redford, leaning up against a worn out desk looking rather plaintive: jacketless, tie partially undone and hanging loosely around his neck, hair mussed. Boyle looks at Redford; Redford looks at Boyle.

Says Redford, "What do we do now?"

Fade out. Roll credits. Please enjoy the buffet. I believe we have some nice egg salad sandwiches and warmish beer for everyone.

After all that. After all the work, the planning, the scheming, and the push, push, push, pull, pull, pull, in the end, all that he could say when it was all over was, "What do we do now?"

See where I'm going with this? Did you see the name of this chapter? Could I be any clearer?

So where do you go from here? Personally I don't have the foggiest idea. I really don't. Of course, if you think about it (and not being able to tell what the future may bring), for the most part, neither do you, except in some ethereal romantic, "I will love you until the day I die" kind of way. And as you sit in your comfortable chair, still reading this book and petting that cat, you may be pondering that same question. Of course, you may also just be pondering if there's any of that mint chocolate ice cream left.

I know one thing though: You definitely do not want to go from here to here in your marriage anytime soon. All I'm saying is that you really don't want that heady rush you have both gotten from your recent experience of falling in love, deciding to take "the big step," planning the entire event, then actually doing it, to ever fade away. Like all other married couples, you are hoping that your feelings of utter completeness and high temperatures of love and commitment stay eternally at the same level of intensity.

Well, they do.

And they don't.

Like just about everything else in life, these feelings and emotions mutate along the journey. Sort of like in the movie, "The Thing." (Not the one with Joel Edgerton, which sucked, but the one with Kurt Russell, which did not suck).

Now, mutation is not necessarily a bad thing. Of course, that dog in the beginning of "The Thing," that was bad, I mean really bad. Bad. Just really, really bad. But mutation is just a way of expressing that over time, everything changes. And to be successful with anything, we/you change with it. You adapt, you accommodate, you overcome.

Your love for your spouse will show itself in many ways and take on many new forms throughout the course of your marriage. Ask anyone who has come through decades of marriage about this and you will get many similar answers: "At the core, the love I first had for my spouse remains the same. But I have learned to show it so much differently now. I'm just better at it. We're just better at it."

I also know a second thing about where you go from here: The path you take, both individually and collectively will ultimately be your own. Through all the motherly and motherly-in-law advice, in spite of folks such as myself or others who write books and produce videos, regardless of where careers and children take you: The path you take with your spouse will be your own, nobody else's.

And that's a good thing.

Before we get to all of the mutation stuff, I am once again obliged to make some clear delineation here. I don't want to confuse any issues, so some kind of clarification needs to be made.

Back in the day, most newlyweds did not live together before marriage. For example, back in the 60's and 70's, the figure that I run into the most is that roughly 10% of men and women lived together without the benefit of marriage (most of them being college kids). It just wasn't something one did. It was only after the marriage that living together was truly acceptable. Nowadays it is much more acceptable and commonplace that a man and a woman can live together without a license from the state. It is more of an individual choice rather than a societal one.

To cite some interesting statistics from some government social scientist somewhere who did some study of cohabitation between 2006 and 2010, one in four women began living with a man outside of marriage by the age of 20. The number rose to three out of four by women in their 30s.

The study goes on to say that 48% of women between 15 and 44 moved in with their man for the first time. Among all age brackets, 40% of those living together ended up marrying within three years, 32% stayed the same, and 27% simply dissolved.

All this means is that many of you I have been addressing in this book may have already been living under the same roof for quite some time before the marriage took place. So you may have a different slant on the problems and pitfalls of sharing the same space. You know, the hackneyed, "Been there. Done that," thing.

For others of you reading this, you may be experiencing living away from college roommates or parents for the first time in your life now that you are married. So you may have no slant on what to expect. You know, the hackneyed, "Huh?" "What?" "Really?" "YOU FRIGGIN DID WHAT?" thing.

All I can say to that is, for any of you who may have been living together for some time before marriage, don't be fooled or complacent. Trust me, no matter how long you may have lived with one another before you took your vows, you must admit that waking up the first morning after marriage was a bit different than the other days. We'll talk about some interesting statistics about all of that in a few moments.

My Advice? Men, pay attention. You ignore this advice at your own peril.

The first discussion about what to have for breakfast. The first discussion on what to watch on TV. The first discussion on "Hey, you going to do the laundry or what? And don't forget to match my socks the way I like 'em." Your first discussion on "Honey, where should we plant the hydrangeas?" Your first discussion on, "What the hell did you feed the cat? And the ever popular, "Hey, what do you think your doing back there? I know we're married, but there will none of that! Wouldn't do it while we were dating, not gonna do it now!" "I hate you."

REAL ADVICE

Even though you may have had them before, these discussions are different after your married. To some of you (those that have lived together) these "firsts" may be subtle, but they're there. For those of you that have not lived together, some of these "firsts" may be quite daunting and things that will probably catch you off guard at some point.

Author's Note: For the purposes of all of us getting out of this book alive, (as well as finishing it all up in this century) for the most part, I am just going to pretend that the advice I give to ALL of you, both the premarital cohabitationers and the newbies, fits you both (Yes, just like a cheap suit.). I will, however, from time to time let the veterans know that I may be covering old ground and that you may leave the room and grab a sandwich or something.

I will also be using the word spouse a lot, except when it's important to make a distinction between males and females. Why? Because it's easier for me if I don't split you up into sexes. Remember the cheap suit thing.

For now, everybody listen up. I wouldn't be doing my job if I didn't briefly mention some additional interesting facts about cohabitation before marriage, and whether that gives anyone a leg up regarding success in your marriage vis-à-vis those who didn't. Please bear in mind that, while I should footnote all of this, I won't. Look it up yourself, or just trust me on blind faith. There will be no exams.

So here we go.

Actually, the statistics on living together before marriage are a mixed bag in regards as to how it may or may not affect any future marital success. Do the research and you get a lot of figures in the 50% range either way, plus a lot of information that doesn't pertain to what brought us all together today. You will also find that there are vast differences whether you're reading a secular or non-secular interpretation of the data (Fox or MSNBC). What does that mean? Mostly nothing. It's just that the Social Scientists and talking heads haven't figured it all out yet.

But still, some cool information can be extrapolated from the data (I am so sorry about that, but if one is going to talk about statistics and statistical information, one must use the words extrapolate, statistical outliers and data. It's obligatory. Mmmm, yes, obligatory).

The reasons for cohabitation are pretty much the same reasons now as they were fifty years ago when only a statistically small percentage of singles (about 10%) were doing it.

In no particular order:

It's cheaper for both.

It becomes a hassle to keep driving back to your place every night so you sort of fall into it.

You truly enjoy each other's company and you find it all so comfortable.

It gives a glimpse into the future.

It helps you "test drive" the relationship.

It will help you "bond." Should you decide to get married, it will make the transition easier.

Sex is ALWAYS close by. All you need now is some Cheese Whiz, and your all set.

REAL ADVICE

And the biggest reason of all: It allows each one of you to sort out problem areas outside of marriage, but within the confines of sharing a space. Even though your not married, you just can't go back to "your place" to cool off. You don't have one. You learn to work it out. You learn to compromise.

Some more interesting facts about cohabitating before marriage include (Again, you can check out these statistics on your own should you desire, but as I said at the outset, there won't be any tests, so.)

Just about 30-40 years ago, "living in sin," as it used to be called had about 500,000 members. Now it has millions (actually, by most accounts, over 7 million). My God, what would Grandma say? Somewhere between 60 to 70 percent of all married couples will have shared a living space prior to marriage.

A lot of research is finding however, that couples who lived together before marriage actually have a higher rate of divorce than couples who don't cohabit before marrying. And before that divorce, these couples had lower rates of marital happiness and shall we say, Customer Satisfaction. "Huh? you say. How can this be? If I'm not happy when I'm living with someone, what in the hell makes me think I'll be happier if I get married to him/her?"

Valid question. Good self-evaluation.

Well, if you didn't believe in the "slippery slope" before reading this, maybe you should revisit it all. It's likely that couples who live together before marriage could be getting married because they're just too damn lazy to "unslippery slope" their way out of it. I mean, you both signed the lease, you got that dog/cat that nobody ever seems to feed, and one of you purchased a cute little teddy (which really looks good on him when he's alone and modeling it in front of the mirror). There is a certain fatalistic quality about it all.

Interestingly enough, couples who moved in together after getting engaged but before getting married are a bit more successful than those who just want to test-drive the relationship. Again, "Why?" you ask? Hell if I know. But if I were to guess, I would say that the former group who move in together after announcing their engagement have already made a conscious decision about the marriage thing. Their commitment is stronger.

Women are more prone to think of moving in together as a prelude to a more solid commitment, while men are thinking more about the short-term advantages, i.e. the distance between sex and beer just got a whole lot shorter. Plus, it does allow him to put off another commitment thing, doesn't it?

Lastly, and if you are a woman reading this, (And you probably are, because what man is going to read about directions for handling a successful marriage?) if you lived with more than one guy during any part of your single life, (First of all, congratulations on that) the chance for divorce can be double that of a woman who did it only once. Why? Again, what the hell do I know? But if I were to hazard a guess on this as well, I would say that it's like killing someone. The first time must be really, really hard. Subsequent killings get a lot easier. Please, don't take me literally on this. Seriously, please just stop it. And no, I will not tell you where that shovel is. Stop.

What I am saying here is that through the lens of having gone through a relationship that simply wasn't working, you have seen the warning signs and are now better equipped to know what will work in the long term and what will not. What is truly salvageable and what is not. You are definitely wiser. This is that, "Been there. Done that" thing I wrote of earlier.

Because this is starting to sound like a high school book report, let me finish with:

One thing that men and women do agree on (finally) is that their standards (such as they are) for a live-in partner are lower than they are for a spouse. Go figure.

Expectations. It always goes back to those, doesn't it?

CHAPTER FOUR

Here's What We're Gonna Do

Because my style of writing is more in the narrative, I need to construct the following chapters and sections a little bit differently than what you may have seen in other books of this type. Don't want anybody to get lost, or worse, angry and confused: "Oh, wait, I thought he said, 'Yes, do go find the shovel and hit...'" Can't have that, can we?

My Advice? It's important that you take into account some of the things that happened in your courtship as well as in your marriage: If you lived with your spouse before you got married. If you had sex with your spouse before you were married. If you both decided to merge your money matters before you were married. If you both managed to solve the toilet seat thing, and who refills the toilet paper roller thing, and whether the end of the roll should hang over top or from underneath, before or after the wedding. Personally, I really hope you solved the whole bathroom thing before you both walked down the aisle. Otherwise, you will probably spend the next decade on this issue and quite possibly, this disagreement will be the trigger for some other unrelated pent up hostilities that have been locked away for a bit. We'll get to that. Again, be patient.

REAL ADVICE

I also need to take into account the newbies that may be in our audience today. Some, maybe all of the aforementioned items may be ones that you haven't gotten to yet, or considered, or are currently going through and need some help and advice.

So we're gonna divide all of this up and mostly talk about the "first" before you were married, then that same "first" after you were married. Even if you have experienced a lot or all of the things I will list before you got married, when they happen after your married, they're different.

I also have to take into account those of you who are reading this book who are not yet married, but have come here seeking some kind of salient solutions and sage advice to sort out any potential problems you may be faced with come the big day.

See all the potential pitfalls from all the potential combinations?

God, all these allowances that need to be made because of the almost infinite variety of living arrangements are really a hassle, but necessary. I really need to double my rates.

Again, so we can get done with this book sometime in the prime of your youth, I have picked out five scenarios that will invariably come up in the first part of your marriage. I promise, I will publish a second book covering five more. Just drop me a line.

Each chapter will be divided into two parts: The first part will concern itself with "events" that happened before you were married, and the second part will deal with those same "events" after you got married. We'll take a look at how you may have handled them as opposed to how you could have handled them differently or should have handled them now that you are married or about to be.

One of the benefits of all of this dividing is to help you and your partner plan for events before you get married. That way, most of the potential obstacles to a successful marriage can be circumvented before your union takes place. It's boring and not very sexy, but it represents good planning on both of your parts.

But why do we look back to the events that may have cropped up prior to marriage, especially if we are mainly interested in moving forward? Because my little Chalamila, past behavior can be a strong predictor of future problems. Remember what Shakespeare said in "The Tempest" (Act 2): "The past is prologue." My apologies. I'm just showing off here.

You will have to be honest with yourself and rather introspective as you read these next chapters. Try to keep in mind that you really can't change everything about the other person in your life. Nature is a powerful thing after all.

Lastly in all of this, you can use this portion of the book as your road map and reference guide, your Rand McNally, as it were, to help keep you on the right road or help you find a way back to a main road. Try as we might, no marriage is immune from falling rocks or cliffs. Falling rocks and cliffs appear because we are human, and as such you will invariably drive off that highway on more than one occasion as you continue on with your life.

Use this book like your Grandma used Dr. Spock's book to figure out your Momma. Keep it in the kitchen by the phone book, or in the workshop, or in that "special" drawer in the bedroom where you keep your "special" things. Don't think I don't know about that drawer.

On second thought, just leave the book in between the recipe books on the kitchen counter. Dog-ear the pages that pertain to persistent problem areas in your marriage and refer back to them when necessary.

Anyway, just follow along here. I will lay everything out so that, yes, even ditzy Bubba can read this and understand it without accidentally lighting fire to it or carelessly dropping it into the toilet.

Just stay calm and you'll be fine. In case you find yourself drifting, I left my private phone number at the end of this book. Call me.

CHAPTER FIVE

It's All About The Firsts

Please note that this is the first part of the five scenarios (events) I will be covering. I'm starting with this inevitable event because in and of themselves, arguments, disagreements, fights, or whatever you want to call them have the potential to loom rather large over your relationship and the first fight over anything at any time can set the tone for many other events including all subsequent fights (or potential fights) no matter what the rest of your fights are about. Therefore, we need to cover this thing first.

The First Fight Before Marriage

Chances are, most of you have already had your first fight long ago, long before you got married. It could have been when you were in high school, college, on a city street corner, at her house, at his house, even on the job. But somewhere, sometime, for some reason, if you are human, you had an argument with your partner.

Now think back. If you have to close your eyes and meditate or do the "Omm" thing, fine. Just go back to that place in time.

REAL ADVICE

For most of us, the exact details of that first fight, for at least one of you, are a bit hazy in your mind's eye: What exactly it was all about, how long it lasted, how far off the main concourse you travelled, how it ended, maybe where it took place, or why it took place at all. While many of the salient details may have been forgotten, as both of you moved on through the months or years together, some of the details (both words and deeds) remain in your head.

You can tell a lot about a person by the way he/she argues. In the course of the argument, did he/she lay his/her hands on you? Was he/she even a tad violent? Did this violence manifest itself verbally or physically, or both. Did he cry? Did she cry? Was cursing involved? Did one of you throw things, or destroy something? Did the words, "Slut, Whore, Bitch" come out of someone's mouth? Did the words, "Weakling, Bastard, Sonofabitch" show up? Was the argument solved then and there, or did you break up and get back together? Was there much screaming and insulting? Did one of you get WAY too personal and go over that line?

There's more to these fights, of course. Lots more. But I think you get the idea.

Having the first fight of your relationship is not necessarily a bad thing. In fact, (within reason) I highly recommend it. First and foremost, it will tell you how the other person acts in moments of great stress. It will also tell you what his or her verbal skills are like. It will also give you some insight into their version of logical thinking and how they process information. Finally, it will tell you what the ground rules will be for the next one, and any modifications that need to be made.

Most important things first: If anyone got violent in any way during this, or subsequent, arguments, watch out. On this one, the statistics are pretty alarming.

Well over one million people will be abused by their partner this year alone. Eighty-five percent will be women; the rest will be men (that's 15%, guys). It is one of the most infrequently reported crimes and some estimate that there are over 3 million each year that go unreported. One in five high-school girls are affected by this violence, but the women who are in most danger are in the 20-24 year old range. And worst of all, it has been estimated that between 40 and 60 percent of those who commit this kind of violence will repeat. Among all of the scary statistics, that one is the scariest.

I completely understand that possibly the first fight took place some time ago, and you were younger then. Passion, especially teenage passion, runs rather high and hot (the hormonal thing). Plus, we're human, and stupid stuff comes out of our mouths all of the time. But while you may be able to "fix" other problems in your relationship, this is the most dangerous one to start with. How many times can you stick your hand inside the lion's cage and not pull out a stump?

Author's Note: As a personal aside (if I may take a moment here), it has always bothered me that those who study this phenomena continue to call it "Spousal Abuse" or "Domestic Violence" or some other catch-all phrase. They do it mostly because it's rather inclusive and encompasses both genders at once since men can be the victims of it, too. The terms also make no distinction whether the abuse is verbal or physical. But years ago, it used to be called "Wife Beating," and the perpetrator who did it was called a "Wife Beater."

REAL ADVICE

To my ears, the terms "spousal abuse," "domestic violence" or any all-encompassing term akin to them should be banned and replaced with the old style stuff. When you were a kid, and you heard that Mr. Jennings down the street was a wife beater, it left absolutely no question in your mind what kind of guy Old Man Jennings was. So, after hearing that, you never ever went close to his house ever again, even on Halloween. In your kid's mind, he was like an axe murderer or something. It's just that the term "wife beater," although rather archaic and not inclusive, is much more on point and so much more descriptive than, "Did you hear about Mr. Jennings down the street? He was just accused of domestic violence."

It's like "serial killer" instead of "mass murderer" or "pedophile" and "child abuser" instead of "child molester" and "monster." To me, the softer terms just don't always convey what they need to.

When my mother died, it was called an, "Unforeseen cardiac event." Now I appreciate the good doctor's attempt to couch his language by using a softer description of her passing, but it took me a moment to fully grasp that for some unexplained reason, her heart stopped beating and she died. The words, "Unforeseen cardiac event" didn't precisely describe the finality of it all.

It's like someone falling out of a 9th story window: "The individual suffered from an acute and pernicious case of 'deceleration trauma' that caused the cessation of all bodily functions." Okay, thank you, but is he dead or what?

As I have already said, and will say again many, many times, we are all human, and as such, will do the exact opposite of what we know we should or what the professionals tell us we should. For no matter how much you study or practice with relationships, when it's finally your turn, you are just as likely as the next person to forget your lines and start making it up as you go along.

All of us have a temper, and all of us can, under stress commit violent acts to one degree or another. Even those guys who sit around all day, contemplating the universe, and catching flies with chopsticks. And yes, even the Dalai Lama said that, "If someone has a gun and is trying to kill you, it would be reasonable to shoot back with your own gun." Of course, the ending to that statement which is rarely quoted, finishes off with, "Not at the head, where a fatal wound might result. But at some other body part, such as a leg." After all, the Dalai Lama is the Dalai Lama. Someone sent that to me on my Facebook page once, and I checked it out myself to verify its veracity. It turns out to be true. Imagine that.

Likewise, Mahatma Gandhi stated in his autobiography, "Among the many misdeeds of the British rule in India, history will look upon the Act depriving a whole nation of arms, as the blackest ... if we want to learn the use of arms, here is a golden opportunity."

No, no one is advocating shooting someone in the leg or head. What I am saying is that, with regards to acts of violence (like acts of bravery), you don't know what you're capable of until you're actually face-to-face with it.

Remember, there are different degrees of violence. Things can start out slowly and subtly, but escalate if a clear line in the sand is not established.

So, if one of you slammed their hands down on the table during that first fight, or banged some pots and pans together, slammed a door or two and stomped in and out of the room with a wooden spoon in their hand, yelling, "And another thing," these actions are frustrations exhibiting themselves, or one of you feels the need to be emphatic and let the other know that you are really quite angry at the moment. But they don't tell us as much as some folks would have you believe. They can be, however, warning signs if they are done to intimidate you, scare you, or in any way make you feel uncomfortable. If the hands being slammed down are fists, put through a wall or a wall close to your body, or that rattling of pots and pans means that one of them will be flying at your head real soon, now those could be precursors to more direct violence.

That last one, the one with the wooden spoon, is done mostly by Irish and Italian women. The French women do it too, but man, if they do it with that accent...

Sorry, sorry. I just needed to lighten it up a bit here.

Now as you are thinking back to those times (and I really hope your eyes aren't actually shut here) how did you diffuse the situation? Did you immediately leave without any further discussion? Did you inform the other person that you'd come back after he/she calms down? Did you stay and using your softest voice in an attempt to talk him/her down? Did you use humor or a hammer? Did you stand up to him/her as you would the schoolyard bully? Did you accept your fate as part and parcel of the relationship?

Man, there are a lot of choices here, aren't there?

Ummm, in case you are wondering, pick the first one. Are you listening? Go with the first thing on the list. Remember, this is an "Advice" book.

My Advice? Get out.

"But what if he/she doesn't hit me? What if I get pushed, or grabbed, or something, that stops short of an actual punch."

My Advice? Get out.

You are right. There are those degrees of aggression. So, let me say this about those possible scenarios: Ummm, in case you are wondering, let me repeat once again: pick the first one. Are you listening? Go with the first thing on the list. Remember, this is an "Advice" book.

If you noticed, the above paragraph was pretty much just a copy and paste job. My advice does not change because you are second guessing yourself or rationalizing his or her behavior. If you are looking down the barrel of escalating violence, and you are feeling the littlest bit hinky about all of this; scram. Figure it all out later. For now, just get to high ground.

Get out. Just turn on your heels, and without taking anything with you, (Except the cat. Take the cat. You know why.) Go to the door and get out. Slam it all to hell if it makes you feel better, but go *now*.

But what if...?

Stop asking yourself those kinds of questions.

I cannot stress this enough. You are either the boyfriend or girlfriend. You are not a psychiatrist trained in talking someone down from the ledge. Once the escalation begins and some bells and whistles go off in your head, you are no longer competent in exactly what to do next. You have just walked out on stage naked. You have just been caught as a party crasher. You have just been given some strontium 90 and are told, "You know what to do with it." The worst thing you can do is ask the, "But what if...?" question. It only serves to help begin the rationalization process.

OK, so you left. Now what. Well, that's up to you. Whether you go back or not is completely your choice. Remember, you own your feelings. Obviously, if this did happen to you, you both worked this particular problem out, and went ahead with your relationship (I know this mainly because you're reading this book). Just always remember that there is a 40-60% chance that at sometime in the future, it's quite possible that it will happen again. If those odds are manageable to you, then the decision on what you do is a forgone conclusion.

Let me leave this part of your first fight with this: "Honey, I promise, if you take me back, I will stop drinking." "No. Stop drinking and I'll take you back." So now we are back to the, "What kind of tree are you?" question.

As I said earlier, that first fight will not only set the tone for future fights, but will also give you powerful insights about what kind of person you are dealing with outside of the ring (if not yourself).

My Advice? Watch for your partners "Tells."

By the way, for those of you unfamiliar with the word "tell," it is a poker term that describes any physical reaction (body language) or kind of behavior, that "tells" the other players how good or bad your hand may be. If you learn the most common tells, you can not only watch your own behavior to make sure your body language isn't telling all of your secrets, but also watch for the habits in the other poker players you're playing with. If you really pay attention to these tells, you'll make much better decisions to hold or fold and maybe win more money. That's why you see so many card players on the World Series of Poker wearing sunglasses and hoodies, looking like the Unibomber.

For the most part, your opponent doesn't even know that he is doing it, but a careful watcher can always pick up the signs. Does he always lick his lips when he is holding a great hand? Does he tug on his ear when he's got nothing?

Everyone with me here? Good, now I'll raise you $20,000, and give me three... tug tug...

Many experts will tell you many things about how to "measure" your future or newly acquired mate (his or her "tells"). For me, the important measure is this: Your observations of your partner's social interactions with others and how he or she handles stressful situations— especially stress.

How does he/she interact with friends? With his or her parents? With the wait staff? With animals? With business/work associates? These are all very important tells and they give you great insights into how his/her mind works or will work in future interplay.

Ah, but fights, arguments disagreements—pressure situations—that's where the real truth about your mate comes out, and not just fights, but any situation that causes them a great deal of stress and consternation. I'm talking about those real human emotional fight or flight moments in all of our lives. This is where your powers of observation are essential in being able to read your partner.

REAL ADVICE

I am not going to pretend, or look past the fact that you are not an infallible creature, and that in times of stress you may need a little help.

Many of us advice givers will tell you, "To start with, should you find yourself in any stressful situation, you should do these three little things..." But under stress, (and being human) we are probably not going to get our pencil out and make a list, or count to whatever, or summon up the best imitation of our indoor voice: "Now I hear what you are saying, and I'm feeling your pain..."

Besides, in many times of great stress, you simply can't go to the nearest referee and call a 30-second time out. Most of us, instead of doing and saying the right and appropriate thing will just snap—to one degree or another—but we'll just snap.

We'll slam the pots, we'll throw the wrench, we'll stomp, we'll slam the door, and we'll walk away only to storm back in again with renewed energy after we thought of that great comeback we just missed five minutes ago. We'll let go with a bunch of stuff we've been saving up for moments like this, we'll say something bad about your mother, we'll mutter some real gangsta stuff under our breath, only to end up with the piece de resistance: guerilla warfare: passive-aggression. BURN them potatoes. "I hate you."

Watching your partner or intended partner go through his or her interactions with the teller at the bank, or the rusty bolt that won't come off, the long line at Golden Corral, or the phone conversation he or she is having with the call center in India while he or she tries to figure out which buttons to push to get the satellite dish activated again, and it's the 4th quarter and your beloved team is down by four with under two minutes to play and they are in the flippin'

Red Zone, and "Gary" from India is telling you to press this button and enter that code and JesusChristAlmighty, I'll just go to my neighbors house and force him to watch the end of the game with me and deal with the inevitable cops situation later, and I've been meaning to make friends with him anyway. Hope he's got the beer I like.

Whew.

We are all dealing with a lot of stuff. We are all fighting our own little battles. But our own observations of how our partners handle these little peccadilloes can give us years of information about the future in just minutes. Like instant pudding. And who doesn't like instant pudding?

If he cried during the first fight, what the hell...? I know it's a stress and tension reliever, but...what the hell? Did he stomp off into the bedroom and play his Josh Groban CD while dusting off his Hummel figurines? All this could very well mean that he is, and will be for some time, a "mommas boy" and has a weak character. Just as importantly, it could be a totally fake act designed to engender some kind of sympathy (especially if he was losing the argument). Either way, he's being a dumb ass. You may call him on this one to get him to shape up. Do not however, during this shaping up portion, use the term, "momma's boy." That would be guaranteed to have the complete opposite effect because now he has to prove what a man he is.

Did she cry? Possible tension/stress reliever? Possible sadness? Perhaps she was thinking that the relationship is over or at least mutated in a not-so-happy way. More likely than not, he said something extremely hurtful that he has said to his guy friends a million times and doesn't have a clue as to what is upsetting you. Forgive him for that one. He really doesn't have a clue. But this is actually fixable.

REAL ADVICE

This is not his nature coming out; it's his nurture. He can be made aware of his insensitivity and correct it.

Yay, a win for you.

My Advice? As you are observing your partner going through all of these stressors or simple human interactions, it is imperative that you keep your own, "I would have done/said it this way," opinions to yourself. You do not have your partner's nature or nurture. It's what you see in them that's important, not necessarily what you would have done faced with the same set of circumstances. It's better to say, I dunno. Maybe you could try this..." and leave it at that.

By the way, and you may laugh all you want, (and I kind of hope you do, I mean, maybe not now, but later, when there are more funny parts) but if the woman is crying during a fight, and she sees that he is getting turned on by this, this is not a good telltale sign. It is a bad telltale sign. While she is crying, he is winning. Whether the argument points he is trying to make are valid or not, he's got you on the run, and as a male, the predatory side will come out in him and now he has grabbed the power. Some males (and this is absolutely true) will actually get an erection if his girlfriend/spouse cries during an argument.

Check it out for yourself if you feel you have a need to. And if you do, and it is so, grab him by his nether region that's now pointing straight at you and don't let go. Just keep a tight hold and swing him around your head like a ten-year-old who's flingin' a cat. Then, at a certain point, just let him go and measure the distance. It's a power thing on his part, so watch it. This kind of guy will never stop making you match his socks and putting them in the dresser drawer just so. I know this falls into the nurture category, but it has a really powerful pull. Hint: It's a mother-son thing.

My Advice? Don't really do that. I mean it's sometimes nice to envision yourself doing that, but really, no, don't do it.

The interesting thing is that the woman can cry during a movie or when watching Animal Planet and an alligator bites the head off of some cute Eland, and nothing from him in the way of a sexual nature. In fact, while being a bit sympathetic and possibly wanting to comfort you, he'll probably just sort of laugh at your "silliness" and move on. But cry during a fight? Turn on? Be warned.

The first fight at any time can be a real mess. Neither one of you really knows what to expect. You are now back to your other "first time," fumbling around in the backseat of your old man's Chevy. Where are the boundaries? How far can I go? How far will either of us go? "You sound just like your father." "You sound just like your mother." "How long do these things last? I mean, damn, The Voice is coming on soon, and yeah, I could eat." "I just am absolutely GodDamn right and why can't that idiot see it, and I'm exhaustipated from all of this. So, should I just give in and wait for another time when the conditions are better? Christ, am I now going to have to plan out future arguments like some modern day Sun Tzu?" "I hate you."

Of course, most lovers' quarrels do not end in some kind of nuclear exchange. Most are handled right then and there, or in a day or two, with residual anger (like radiation fallout) possibly lasting a bit longer.

All in all, regarding the fights or arguments or discussions before marriage, there are some exit options. You can exit stage left temporarily, or take a bow and exit never to be seen or heard from again. You can go back home, or back to your dorm. Going to see Patty or Tom is another option. Or, you can stick it out all the way, come to terms with your partner, patch it all up and go on with your lives.

My Advice? Two things: Patience and objectivity. Once again, there's a lot more components that could be thrown in, and most advice givers will produce a list comprised of at least ten, but if you can start with those two, you will find that having both of those properties will serve you quite well over time. And remember, with any subsequent arguments, you will both improve your game.

Often, we let so many things build up in our system like toxic waste. It's the toilet that we don't always flush. All that waste builds up until the whole sewer line fails under the pressure and the inevitable backflow occurs. I wish I could convince you to always stay calm under stress, but we both know that human reactions don't always work that way.

But, I do want to convince you that trying this patience thing and the objectivity thing is truly worth your while. They are powerful tools that will help you cope with just about any argument that you and your partner will occasionally partake in.

Let me start this patience part with the following little ditty. It's an old saying, but it bears repeating: "It's better to keep your mouth shut and appear stupid than open it and remove all doubt." Mark Twain said that. I'm not sure it's totally on point, but it'll have to do.

Now, if your partner comes at you with a complaint, or especially a series of complaints, he or she has let some toxic waste build up in his or her sewer lines. And he or she has picked this exact moment to flush. Regarding the timing of this, you have no control. Patience is the key here.

Think about it, if this were you doing the flushing, you may start to unload on your partner the same way he or she is unloading on you. So be patient and listen. Don't speak. Don't interrupt. Let your partner get out all the bad humors.

Many times the issue(s) your partner is hurling at you have been simmering in the pot for a while now, and no matter how many discussions with friends, family and/or coworkers he or she has had up until this time, he or she has not yet approached you about it (them). And frankly, you are the only one that matters. Telling or complaining to others is just practice. All that has come before this has been a series of dress rehearsals for the real thing. In sports parlance, it's spring training.

So here's your partner flushing any toxins out of his or her sewer lines. While it may not be the most pleasant experience you have ever gone through, stand your ground, make constant eye contact, nod your head when you must and don't interrupt. It is so critical that you let your partner finish his or her complete thoughts. Otherwise, the issue(s) not only become much more important than they should, other, more divergent and esoteric issues arise. The discussion could go on all night, and there's work tomorrow.

The point is, nobody, including you, likes to be interrupted when presenting a complaint or two. Sometimes it takes a bit of courage and rehearsals before you are confronted. Let your partner get it out. You are not placating or patronizing. You love this other person, and along with this love you have respect. So respect. Have patience. Just listen until you are sure everything about the issue is out.

Now, like the bottle on your bathroom counter says, "Rinse and repeat." Repeat back to your partner what was just said. Do not sound like a parrot. Just present the highlights. And please don't preface it all with, "I hear what you are saying..." Your partner will instantly realize that you are doing some reading on the outside and you will have absolutely lost any credibility.

Besides your demonstrating that you were really listening, repeating back your partner's words gives you some much needed time for your brain to begin to formulate an answer that will preserve your dignity as well as managing any possible escalations.

After you have let your partner flush, let the objectivity portion come through. Here is where you find out what kind of tree you really are. Oak? Strong, unyielding. Willow? Bendy, amenable. Wisteria? Just stand there and look pretty. Are you a giver? A taker?

Decide.

Be as objective as you possibly can. Ask yourself, "What do I lose by admitting he/she is right in his/her complaint(s)." "What do I gain by admitting he is wrong?" "If I were him/her, would I feel the same?" And if you have any inkling that your partner may have a point, let him or her know it.

Here are two common scenarios that couples argue over. They are rather simplistic, but for those of us who have been in a relationship argument, we know how easily they can become the mushroom cloud of a nuclear exchange.

He says, "We are always late for everything. You take so damn long to get ready. We're late for parties, the movies, dinner reservations, and church. Damn it girl, I hate it!"

Author's Note: New studies have come out that show both women and men take about the same amount of time to get ready for either work in the morning or a night on the town. Interestingly enough, these same studies also reported that men take just a bit longer to shave than women do. Just sayin'.

Author's Note: There really isn't much empirical evidence in these studies. Most of them merely polled the individuals involved. So, especially in regards to some of the evidence, men realize that there are exactly 60 seconds in each minute, while women believe there are at least 70. Women, it would seem have a greater ability than men to compress time. It's magical. Plus it would solve the mystery of why women can shave all of their places quicker than a man can shave his face.

Admittedly, being late isn't the end of the world, but it could be the end of a pleasant night out. If this little problem isn't handled on the spot, he will speed all the way to wherever you are going and you could all die in a fiery crash. Worse, you could make it all the way to your destination in complete and utter silence. He is in a bad mood not just because you two are late, but because this is the umpteenth time you two have been late, and he is totally sick and tired of it. Sorry, but that's the long and short of it.

You can either accept his anger as his and his alone to deal with and get over, or you can acknowledge his anger and frustration and make your move.

"Yeah, we are late for almost everything, and it takes me a bit of time to get ready because it's important to me that I always look good when I'm out with you. Look, it would help if you make sure that all the housework is pretty much done so that I can start getting ready a little earlier. That would save me so much time. And I promise I will try and be a little faster from now on."

It's worth a try.

Yes, I know, it's pretty simplistic. But the important thing is that your words are comforting and you're not getting in his face. Also, notice how in this scenario, you didn't use the word, "but" as in, "Yeah, we are late for almost everything, but it takes me a bit of time..." No buts. Often the word "but" has a very bad connotation, as in, "I love you but..." Don't use it as there is a chance that your conversation will be, "Yeah, we are late for almost everything, but it takes me a bit of time to get ready because you never do anything around the house and I end up doing it all by myself while you just sit there on your fat ass complaining. Cue the mushroom cloud.

That word "but" while only three little letters carries a ton of weight.

Anyway, the response you gave about the reasons for being late showed that you were listening, showed that you cared about his feelings, and showed that you were being objective. Let us also not forget that you also gave him a little hope in that from hereon, you will try and do better.

You can be the mighty Oak outside the home, but sometimes the Willow is truly the way to go. And you are also the Wisteria cuz you look so pretty.

In the second scenario, she says, "I always know where you've been because everywhere I go, I can follow your trail of used dishes, dirty counters, and clothes all over the floor. Damn boy, I hate it!" This, of course, is probably hyperbole, but what she is saying is that you are a mess and it's been bothering her because someone has to clean up, and it certainly isn't you.

Who is more of a mess (men or women) is much harder to quantify than the lateness thing. Most of the data you can find is anecdotal. ("I'm a mess? Well, let's just dump out your purse and my wallet at the same time and see who is the bigger mess.")

For the most part, it's more of a personality (nurture) thing. But this little discussion has the potential of turning into quite the donnybrook.

Regardless of its causal connection, here we are at the stereotypical mine field: Men are a mess. Women are tidy. Or, more to the point, she sees the male counterpart in her life as a slob.

OK men, your turn under the microscope: Mighty Oak? Willow? Baobab? Albino Redwood? Sorry, but Wisteria is not an option for you. You are simply not, and never will be, "pretty."

The same advice I gave to the woman in your life in the first scenario is the same advice I am now imparting to you: Listen-all the way through.

Author's Note: Listening all the way through may take a while, as it has been reported in the Journal of Neuroscience that women have more of the FOXP2 protein than men. FOXP2 is commonly called the

"Language Protein" and it is the biological reason why women talk more than men (20,000 words per day as opposed to 7,000 words each day by men.).

Some folks, as well as some researchers, still call this word count disparity a myth. Personally, I say, "Who cares?" There's no value judgment on the number of words each sex says every day.

But there is one thing I do believe in all the word counting: Women, more than men, converse more in the "feeling/emotional" spectrum while men converse more in the "information dissemination" spectrum.

What that means is that more often than not, you will not only hear about your slovenly behavior, but an entire litany of ways it makes her feel as well. Again, let her finish. Don't interrupt. Besides, letting you know how this behavior affects her emotionally is not a negative thing. In its own way, it truly helps to clarify her argument.

Patience. Patience. Patience.

Again, just like my previous advice, paraphrase back to her what she just said (Not the emotional part yet, just the you being messy part.).

Let her know you were listening and you really do care about how that makes her feel. Chances are, you are a slob. After all, she may have seen your college dorm room.

Now is the time to be really, really objective. Are you messy? Do you make messes? If you think about it, at least some of the time you leave a mess wherever you go. Admit it. "Yeah, I am a mess sometimes, and I'm sorry it makes you feel bad. I'll do better." That's simple, direct, and to the point. This is what your partner wants to hear. And think of it this way: In your answer to her complaint, you have used less than 1% of your daily allotment of 7,000 words. Resourceful and economical. Now do it; clean up after yourself.

My Advice? Do NOT ask to see her purse, the back seat of her car or her side of the closet. Don't tell her she talks too much. Do not stray from the specific point she is making about what a mess you create as you move from one room to another. It will only end up in disaster. Besides, being messy in the totality of the universe is no big thing. Dragging this discussion through the mire is simply not worth the toll it will take on both of you. Keeping the house in decent shape is just as much your responsibility as hers and that's what being an adult is all about.

Not to deviate too much, but there was a study done in the U.K. recently that espouses the belief that men reach the age of emotional maturity at about the age of 43. Women, it was noted, reach their emotional maturity much sooner: at age 32.

Among the telltale signs: Grown men continue to laugh about their own burps and farts; they continue to retell the same old stories and still get a laugh from them; beating their children at games; eating fast food after 2 am; and playing practical jokes. The study lists around 20 more signs, and that's a lot of fodder for some excellent guy jokes, but I think I will pass and finish up this for your consideration:

If I'm a guy, calling another guy to let him know I'm going to be late because traffic was so bad on the Howard Franklin, my friend on the other end of the line will probably say, "That's why I'll always take the Courtney Campbell." I'll accept that and drive on.

Now, chances are, if a woman gets that response from her man, this is not necessarily what she wants to hear. Better to respond with, "That's awful. Are you okay? I know traffic on that road can be quite tricky, and the other drivers can be a bit aggressive. Would you like to keep talking to me while you negotiate the traffic (assuming she can do this safely without holding a cell phone)."

I know, my wording is a bit clumsy here, but what I am trying to demonstrate is empathy. "I feel your pain." Empathy and sympathy are two very different things. Sympathy is merely, "Sorry, Dude. See yah when ya get here." Empathy is, "Just remember, I'm right there in the front seat with you."

See the difference?

My Advice? Men, during those times when you are getting complaints from your women, get some damn empathy and use it. Always.

The First Fight After Marriage

So the first fight, the pre-marriage one, is out of the way. Each subsequent fight, argument, disagreement, difference of opinion—whatever you are calling it—has gotten a bit "better." By that I mean any fights after the first, while possibly having their deleterious effects on both of you, have also brought you closer together, and are being managed better. The apologies were really great, as were the promises. The sex was pretty cool as well: bit more passionate, a little more vocal. The post-coital sandwiches were a nice touch and very much appreciated, but can we get some chips for next time?

You have both, in effect, farted in front of each other for the first time.

But the first fight after marriage really is a bit different; It's like winter in Florida: There are no snow drifts or bone cracking winds that will take the side of your face off. But even though it's still 80 degrees outside and your sitting at some Tiki hut having a Cuba Libre in your swimming trunks and that really embarrassing "Bikini Inspector" T-shirt, the hues and intensities of a change in seasons are there if you look close enough.

Actually, another one of my sports analogies is called for here. If you've watched your favorite football team pull ahead of their opponents by, say, two touchdowns, and it's late in the 3rd quarter or early in the 4th, you notice that your team is doing a lot of 3 and outs. No more of the complex offensive schemes you witness earlier. Just dull, ordinary plays. Your team has a decent defense, and it seems as if the coach will be relying on them to lock down their opponents. Even the idiot color commentator notices: "It seems like the (insert your favorite teams name here) are playing more not to lose than they are playing to win."

Sometimes marriage fights are like that. You could be playing too conservatively.

With your fight(s) before marriage, you had lots choices: "OK, I'm outta here. I'm going back to my place—to Pattys—home (if you were living with your parents), to see the boys, etc. And you could do this at least for the rest of the night and probably well into the next day, maybe into the next week.

There's also the one that ALL men just love to hear: "Screw this. Why I ever gave up Thomas for you, I'll never know. I've still got him on speed dial. Maybe I'll give him a call. I hate you." She, of course says this while walking out the door. Men, of course are completely emasculated in the .385 seconds it takes a major league hitter to decide whether to swing at that fastball comin' at him—and curiously turned on at the same time. Strange how the male mind works, isn't it?

One of you could also say, "Look, let's just break up."

In that case, "Let's just break up," means one of three things:

1. You just really want to end the whole thing.

2. You are testing him or her.

3. It just slipped out.

Unless you two have had a series of fights, and it really has gotten profoundly depressing to be around each other and both of you are going through the motions of a relationship but he's too lazy to leave you (plus, you make really great sandwiches) and you are still so sure you can change him and bring him into step with the rest of humanity, please refer to number two.

That's right class, and we do this all the time. Remember the boundary thing? Whoever said one of those above three sentences (the male or the female) doesn't matter. Instead of looking one another in the eyes and asking, "Are things going just a bit too far?" we dare one another. We are back on the playground when we were 10-years-old and finding out just how far someone will go—or not.

Either way, that question about breaking up is a real showstopper, isn't it? Think back to when that statement was directed at you. And at some time in your life it was. It's important that we be honest in these sessions. Most likely, you deflected and after a moment of silence, you answered (all together now): "Well, is that what you want? And the answer is... "Hell no, but if you back down, I own you." And, one of the important boundaries is found. It's a power thing. It's something that the schoolyard bully would do. And once the bully wins, that's the way it will stay.

But that first fight after marriage is not the same, and many of the options I spoke about in the paragraphs above aren't there anymore. No, you can't go home, (if you were still living with mom and dad) or to your place or to Patty's, and it's probably not a very wise decision to give Thomas a call (unless, of course, he's really THAT good.). But if you think about it, for men, "I'm going to see the boys" is still one of the options. Keep in mind however, that this decision will lead him back to the "...making choices..." portion of the Introduction for this book. It's sort of a circle of life thing.

You may be thinking at this moment that, "Hey, I can still go see Patty." No you can't. Patty's at home and her husband is there, and you really hate him right now because he's a good friend of your husband's, and you really don't want to see or deal with any of his idiot buddies right now. (Unless, his name is Thomas, and he still is really that good.)

So what's left? Well, if you have been paying attention like you should, all that's left is the "Do you want to break up?" question. If you hear it from your husband, I guess at this point a small tap on his medulla oblongata with the frying pan wouldn't hurt. "Hey dummy, we're not in high school any more. We are married. The proper term is not " break up." It's, "divorce." As in, "Maybe we should get one."

Who in the hell taught you how to speak? And stop laughing when you are chewing food. Completely gross and makes you look like the special guest star on Duck Dynasty. I mean, they can do it, but not you. And go comb your hair. You look horrible, and I can't argue with you when you look like that." "I hate you."

By acting like "Crazy Cat Woman," you are accomplishing four things when that question comes up:

1. You are standing up for yourself.

2. You are once again deflecting, and turning the tables while totally confusing the poor lad.

3. You are sending him to the bathroom and out of your life for a minute.

4. You are secretly turning him on a bit because you're acting like his mother, and remember that eternal bond between momma and son.

There are a lot of emotions that go along with the first fight after marriage: The most important thing might be a sort of sense of betrayal. And that sense of betrayal can cause a real long turn on the melancholy ride at the fair.

Don't confuse the definition of "betrayal" as the one you use most often. We are not speaking about it's normal usage in the sense that one or the other person in the relationship has betrayed the other by calling up Thomas or by slipping out with the boys on Friday night to attend the buffet bar at Hooters.

No, this betrayal has to do with messin' with the wedding vows. A real roots and dirt thing, chewing at the basic ingredients that made your holy matrimony, well, holy. And that can be much, much worse.

There's always something special about "us." Our union that is about to come, or has just taken place is different from anyone else's we have seen. As a couple, we are different than both our parents, the couple down the street, Sean and Kathleen from college, and of course Kim Kardashian and Ray J (or Kim Kardashian and Kris Humphries, Kim Kardashian and 50 Cent, Kim Kardashian and Nick Lachey, Kim Kardashian and Reggie Bush, Kim Kardashian and Gabriel Aubry, or Kim Kardashian and Kanye West ...). By the way, Kardashian left Aubry because she felt HE was using HER for fame.

Go figure.

Anyway, the union that the two of you have made or will soon make, has not yet been tainted by anything—not a scratch, a blemish or a mark on it. It's that new blender from Wal-Mart. It's clean. It's shiny and new, and feels the way a kitten ought to feel. It smells like it just came out of the dryer.

But like anything else, we have to take it out of the garage, we have to put it on and wear it. We have to plug it in and turn it on. The cat is going to do something really bad to it. In short, your relationship will, like everything else, be field-tested. And sooner or later, well... let's just say, "That's gonna leave a mark."

All of a sudden, that first fight after marriage makes you both mortal again. You see your "perfect" pure relationship brought down a bit from the extra-large fries to the regular-sized order. You can now be lumped in with your parents, the couple from down the street, Sean and Kathleen, and Kardashian and everyone but me.

And it can really make the mood around the house a bit melancholy for a while. But take heart: because you HAVE had a fight or two before this one, and hopefully, both of you are better at resolving your current one. You have been paying attention to the "tells," the triggers, the stressors, and the power plays, so the duration and the intensity have been muted somewhat.

As a male, I always considered dating and cohabitation in my younger days as a sort of spring training, where I could work out the kinks and improve my game so that once I got to the show, I would at least ACT like I knew what the hell I was doing. I know that sounds a bit inarticulate to some of you, but we all approach life in the way that helps us as individuals make sense of it all.

My Advice? Get over it. Don't let it fester. And be verbal about it. You have BOTH fallen a bit short of your ideal. After the dust settles (and it will, I promise) let your partner know in one way or another that it's OK, that you are both human, and as such you are going to do human things—like argue. It's all part of the pageantry, and neither one of you has somehow failed some kind of test. Actually, you have passed. You have come up against one of the deadliest pitfalls of married life—and except for the corresponding dent on the side of his head as the one on the frying pan—no lasting damage was done.

If you are thinking, "Jesus, here I buy this book in the closeout bin hoping for some decent advice and all I get for my troubles is, 'Get over it?' I could have gotten that advice from my mom for free." Well, think about it. What other choice do you have? You want to carry the remnants around with you? What about the next one, or the one after that, or that, or that? It's only going to build up and get heavier and heavier. I promise you, THAT is much worse. This is the perfect opportunity to act like the mighty Oak. Let the prevailing winds do what they will, and after the storm has passed, there you are, standing tall.

Get over it, take the high road, own the thing, and get on with you life (lives).

In case I need to make all of this clearer. Do NOT do this just in your head. Verbalize it. Let your partner know that even though it left a mark, or a scratch, or a dent, it will heal, you will both be the better and wiser for it, and the issue in question has been resolved. And remember—you do NOT lose any points for being the leader in this discussion. It does not take the power away from you. In fact in the recipient's eyes, it makes you stronger. Trust me on this. When you are able to look someone square in the eyes and be honest without rancor and tell them that things got away from both of you, but you have both recaptured it all, your stock improves. The mighty Oak.

Normally I don't like to do this, but let me share a personal anecdote from my life. It didn't involve an argument, but it explains what we are going after here.

As we began to have children (we have four, all females) I, for the first time in my life, began to hold children in my arms. Well, the truth is, I was pretty bad at it. Upon my first several attempts, I was a bit rough and a little too loud when all I was trying to be was all soft and Cheez Whiz melty with them. I did not realize this was what I was doing. I thought I was doing just fine.

REAL ADVICE

Well, my wife saw this, and gently told me to just love her and hold her and not to worry. She did not snatch the baby from my arms, or debase me for being insensitive, or accuse me somehow of being a bad father. She just said it was all right, you're going to do fine, and what a lucky child to have you as her dad.

Talk about taking advantage of a teachable moment. Any fear of my present or future performance as a father pretty much disappeared at that moment and right then and there I learned how to hold and love my child to both of our benefits. It made me stronger. It made me better. And in my eyes, it made my wife stronger. And I am sure it made our child stronger. I have never forgotten that one moment in time. And honestly, I never would have survived fatherhood without going through it.

Teachable moments. Can't say enough about 'em.

One last thing before we leave. Under no circumstances after the dust settles, (and your verbalizing in the "debriefing" portion) make any promises or suggestions you cannot keep. Especially the, "Let's not ever fight again." statement; or the, "I promise I will never throw that frying pan at you again." You are going to fight again. You are going to stomp in and out of a room again, slam things, sulk, say, "...and ANOTHER thing..." purposely burn them potatoes. You are just gonna. Because you are human. And you have emotions. And you have convictions. And they will get in the way and cloud the issues from time to time. And that's OK.

So what makes you different from your parents, the couple from down the street, Sean and Kathleen, and Kardashian and everyone but me?

Well, first of all, you read this book. Secondly, because you read this book, you now find it easier to stop and really listen to your partner and have your partner really listen to you.

Now that you know you are ever so close to deciding what kind of tree you are, let's move on to what all newlyweds face right up front: household finances.

CHAPTER SIX

You Spent How Much On What?

or

What To Do About Finances

There's been a series of TV commercials promoted by a long-range financial planning group. Many of their commercials show a young couple just starting out, and they're supposed to follow a green line. At the end of it (the future) they will find financial security and comfort waiting for them as they effortlessly transition into their golden years.

One of the commercials in the series depicts a young man or woman (I can't remember which) following the line and along the way they spy a really cool sports car that is off of the green line. As he/she makes a hard right turn and approaches the car, a financial advisor magically appears and warns him/her not to step off of the line. Like a chastised child, the client does an about face and continues down the path.

REAL ADVICE

Yes, it's wise that you continue down the road to prosperity with little or no missteps. Yes it's wise not to get yourself and your mate into a possible financial quagmire. And yes, it is extremely important that we all plan for our later years.

But, it is a sports car after all. And it's shiny. And it's fast. And oh so cool. And I'll look really cool driving it. But we all know it's the fruit from the forbidden tree. It cannot be afforded right now. It is not a wise choice. And so, being rational and thoughtful, we will deliberate.

And after your sane deliberations are over, you buy it despite the fact that it is verboten. Why? Because in the final analysis, you rationalize that if you don't get it now, you will only get it when you're old (but financially secure). This will be at the time when you suffer from arthritis, gout, semi-blindness, and extremely poor reflexes. Add to that, all your friends and relatives will believe you're going into your "second childhood." The certainty that you will die in a fiery crash is all but assured. Of course, now that you're financially secure, your spouse will see a hellofa life-insurance payday.

My Advice? All things considered, the sports car is not a wise choice. But it sure is nice to dream, ain't it?

Close to home, there have been many occasions when I have asked my wife to stop at the store on her way home from work to buy a gallon of milk. Three hours later, she'll return home with a trunk full of groceries, at least eight bales of hay (No, we don't eat it; we have horses.) and a new riding lawn mower strapped on the hood.

I discovered years ago that she has no green line. Knowing that, and making allowances for it, how can I ever complain? Besides, I have six really high-tech riding lawnmowers sitting in my yard, and if I can just get a couple more, I can trade them in for that really cool shiny sports car.

Besides sex, what kind of designer clonebaby you want to create or what to have for dinner, figuring out your finances as a married couple has the capacity to wreak complete and utter havoc in your relationship like nothing else. And if you have been one of those lucky couples that have never had a fight in your relationship—your gonna have one hell of one now. You'll want to kill him (Please don't take me literally.). You'll want to kill her (Again, please don't take me literally). Just remember what the Dalai Lama said, "Shoot 'em in the leg."

Both of you will just want to set fire to everything, sew some latex (please check for allergies first) costumes together and go off into the wilderness (maybe Detroit) dressed as Mad Max and Wonder Woman, and fight crime—only because fighting crime in the sewers of a major metropolis that has nothing to lose is so much easier that sitting down with your spouse and saying, "Honey, we need to figure out how we're going to pay...."

Oh, damn.

As usual, let me make sure I'm addressing those I need to be speaking to.

If you've attended one of those money management seminars, or visited somebody's website or blog, or editorial comments page, you probably have found that many address how young couples should be handling their finances, and will attempt to help you by offering a list of helpful hints like: "Three ways to..." or, "Top ten reasons you should..." or, "Are you ready for retirement...?" "How does your portfolio measure up?" "Make a list..." (You really have GOT to find that pencil in the junk drawer.) and so on.

Author's Note: If you are one of those couples who are fortunate enough by birth or by your own industriousness to have copious amounts of dough to divvy up your combined incomes and put it all in several "pots" for your stock portfolio, a joint checking account, individual savings accounts, a college fund for your yet to be genetically designed clonebaby, a little bit for that Cayman Island account, a household budget account, AND the retirement funding so you can totally walk away from it all at 35, ride horses on the beach, and live life like you are in some Cialis commercial, you may skip this chapter.

In fact, if you have ever been to any seminar or anything that even resembles one, (I'm not including Comicon) I will not be talking to you. Please feel free to leave the room, stretch your legs a bit and go get a sandwich. Or better yet, have your butler go get it, or the waiter at the country club where you are currently having lunch. Go on now. There you go. That's right. We'll see you again in a few pages. I will be addressing the rest of humanity. That would be the 98% who own the 2%.

Now I see some of you squirming a little bit, and feeling somewhat insulted; but please, don't be (Well, actually, you can squirm as much as you want to). It's just that we can't cover this part of married life without absolute and brutal honesty. You're young, you're just starting out, the economy sucks, your paycheck sucks, the government sucks, your boss sucks, and no matter what you do, with both your combined incomes, the dollar menu at McDonald's on Friday is about it.).

Oh, and please don't worry. In a little bit I will be passing out some free egg-salad sandwiches for you to munch on. I forget where I got them. I think it was at someone's wedding reception or wake or someplace. Well, I'm sure you'll enjoy them.

One last thing before we start, and I promise this will not be a clone of a Suzi Orman seminar. Fact is, I watched a portion of one of her videos the other day and she was giving advice to some woman on saving for a "rainy day fund." She advised the audience member to put the extra family money into a Roth IRA. This is not bad advice. Later on down the road when you are older and no longer need or want to follow the long green line, you get some money back with interest and some great tax benefits.

She went on to say, rather matter of factly, that a person can contribute up to a maximum of $5,500 each year up to age 50, at which time it can be increased by $1,000 per year. There's a lot of other stuff to consider, plus a whole lot of rules, but I kept thinking to myself that if your combined income is what I think it is right now, 5,500 bucks of unspent money throughout the year is a bit much.

Suzi and that cavernous mouth of her's are right, by the way. If you can squirrel away that much per year, you could put in almost $200,000 by the time you are sixty. Add in the interest, and you've got about a quarter of a mill by the time you can take full advantage of it.

Not bad at all.

Just keep in mind that to accomplish this, you need to have $15.00 a day to contribute each and every day. This includes Saturdays, Sundays and all acknowledged holidays. It doesn't sound like much, but that's $105.00

each and every week; $210.00 every paycheck; $420 each and every month for pretty much the rest of your life.

But Grand-Canyon-sized mouth Orman also said something like, "If you are saddled with student loan debt, find some money to pay it off as soon as possible."

"Find some money." Yeah, you go out and do that right after you hop into your 1986 Oldsmobuick and gas it up with the $3.46 in change you have laying in your cupholder. Sorry, but you don't have the $180,000 to pay off the student loans. And for the foreseeable future, you are sure you can't get your hands on it. It's not under the couch cushions. You couldn't sell enough of your crap on eBay to earn it. Mommy and daddy don't seem to have it either. So unless Ms. Orman has it in her checking account, you are just shit out of luck.

The point is, most seminar givers (with or without the cavernous mouth thing) assume you have money that you are just not applying wisely. Sometimes that's true, but oftentimes it isn't. Most of the nearly newlyweds or just got married newlyweds are busy making sure that rent is paid on time, the electricity doesn't go off, Uncle Sam is pretty happy that you are at least paying something on those student loans, and that the purchase of a jar of spicy mustard will not break the budget.

My Advice? You must be brutally honest with all of this. You may not be able to make any great headway on paying off your student loans (think forbearance). You may not be able to afford $5,500 each year to a Roth IRA. Maybe though, you can afford something, say, $5.00 a day. If so, do it. If not, put it on that to-do list and make sure you get back to it as soon as you figure out all of the finances.

No matter how you may hate to hear it right now, you may be part of the great unwashed, the teeming masses, America's working-class heroes. And as much as you might want to say or think otherwise, you have to be utterly and totally forthright about your current and foreseeable future financial situation. The worst thing you can do here is kid yourself. You will go into the deep end of the pool and your toes will no longer touch the bottom, and you won't have your water wings on, and you'll go under and well, let's just say your presence from hereon in will be sorely missed.

Allow me to illustrate further.

I heard a joke/story the other day told by a Scotsman. So as you read it, it would help if you did it with a Scottish brogue.

"I've seen the winter. Five feet of snow. And here me Grandad was only 4 feet 11. Didn't see him till March."

"Aye, a real tragedy, that."

"Oh, nay. Grandad was a wee bit of a sonofabitch... Grandma was quite pleased."

So your financial size right now may be 4' 11" and your wants and desires (maybe even your needs) are at 5 feet.

My Advice? The best thing to do is admit that and don't venture out into anything that is deeper than your head.

No, you may not be rich. You may not have a lot of money. So why should we spend any time even going over the financial issues?

Well first of all, did you know that couples fight over money more than sex? It's true. At least that's how it was reported

REAL ADVICE

by *Money Magazine* sometime back. Curiously, while couples fight more about money than sex, it's not as much as they fight over simple household chores or children. Hmm.

And we also have to talk about money matters because of the fact that your financials are possibly very limited. Once you get in over your head (see the pool analogy above) it's really, really hard to get your little toes to touch bottom again.

Before we totally immerse ourselves in all this money talk, let's visit how males and females view things in different contexts. I know, I know, but I promise I won't be as boring as you think I will be.

Generally speaking, (I say generally, because it lets me off the hook on so many different levels) men and women can often see the world as two completely different places and subsequently react to the same stimuli differently.

Men tend to measure their version of a successful life by their job (status) and how much money they make (power). They will tell you there is more: power tools, perceived athletic prowess, the number of male offspring they have generated, past success with the ladies, and their ability to begin and end all phone calls in six words or less.

Author's Note: This list is not all-inclusive. There are many elements that could be added in and make a pretty nifty Top Ten or Top Twenty List, but in all honesty, for men, it's usually all about power and money. The rest is pretty much filler.

For women, it's a bit different. They operate on a slightly higher plain. That is not to say women aren't as interested in a buck as the next person, or in making it big in the corporate world. They are. But there is one other element they seem to have at the forefront as to how they measure a successful life, and it's very much tied into how much happiness and joy they have brought to others. Now boys, aren't you ashamed of yourselves?

How does this all tie into managing money (or even discussing it in a manner that won't leave both of you in a bloody mess?). I don't know; that's sort of up to you, now isn't it?

Your Finances Before Marriage

My Advice? Boys, as soon as you get up from bended knee; girls as soon as you put that exclamation mark after the word "Yes!"—before the announcements, before the parties and the plans and the showers and that last little fling with Thomas, go directly to the nearest table with a pad and pencil (that pencil you had to steal from the supply room at work because you have never been able to find the one in your junk drawer) and sit with your meager finances and begin planning. Take care of as much of as much as you can as early as you can. I know it's not as sexy as having your engagement party at The Four Seasons in New York or The French Laundry (That's another hot, trendy restaurant) in California, but you can't afford them anyway. Besides, the rich folks that left the room a while ago have all met there for dinner, so there's a really long wait.

Look, what I said a few paragraphs above is true: men and women are going to see this financial thing in different ways, and you will too. At some point, you will disagree. That's fine. You think any bank or corporate merger, no matter how big or small, isn't without its hiccups? You will have yours, so it's better to do it early and in stages.

REAL ADVICE

Remember, no matter how much money they both have (or don't have) individually or pooled together, men and women can have totally different ideas about who does what with the soon to be family money, and what their partners care about. Husbands (or fiancés) can be especially clueless, (sorry) because they don't always get how much women care about almost every financial issue, from saving for retirement to paying off debt. Women come much closer in understanding what matters to men. If anything, they tend to give guys way too much credit, believing their man cares more about paying off debt (like that Vizio 58 inch 21:9 Widescreen HDTV with the 900 channels he just bought) and saving for big purchases (like another Vizio 58 inch 21:9 Widescreen HDTV with the 900 channels for the bedroom) than guys actually do.

Basically, we are back to the Rand McNally thing. Women will stop at the gas station and ask for directions. Once they've taken the step of seeking advice, they tend to listen and take action.

Oftentimes women, unlike their male counterparts, are comfortable with the long view. They focus on how spending, saving and investing can support their life goals.

Notice I just said "life goals" here. They are life goals because they are probably not "right now goals" because you still ain't got no money. But you will, (I believe in you, my little Babushka) and planning for that time is not wasted motion by any means. So, dare to dream.

And here's where it goes back to the beginning: For women, money is about a lifestyle (happiness and joy), while for men it can be more about winning and losing (status and power).

But still, even here in the more enlightened 21st Century, husbands and wives divvy up money-related issues and tasks along very traditional lines. Men still tend to do most of the big-picture, long-term planning while women manage the household's day-to-day finances. Women want to know "Are we on that little green line?" Their concerns often include the day-to-day management of whatever assets there are. They're more end-result oriented, whereas, for example, men tend to be more concerned about issues such as, "What are the rates today, and are we in a Bear or Bull Market?" Yeah, like he watched CNN Money Matters one time, and now he's an expert:

> Sir Larry Wildman - Wall Street
>
> Bluestar. Don't make a big deal.
>
> Buy it lightly on the way down.
>
> (emphatically) When it hits 18—buy it all.

Author's Note: Now again, I'm aware that I am addressing many different types of individuals with colorful backgrounds and life experiences. Some of this pertains to the fact that maybe you just got married, or you are about to; whether you have been living together or not; whether a child is involved or not; and so on. So I will do my best to cover the rest of this financial stuff the best I can without making you think that I think you are an idiot.

First off, always, always, always look for the "tells." And here is where the nurture part of your partner comes into play. Remember, both of you were raised in separate households, and quite possibly were exposed to completely different ideas about the value of money and success. Always keep in mind that when discussing finances, your future mate will more often than not, be coming from a much different place.

REAL ADVICE

My Advice? Be sensitive to this. Take into account the philosophical differences concerning money between the two of you. He may have grown up in the home I first cited in Chapter One, (not so fortunate) while you may have grown up in home number two (very blessed). Before any final commitments are made that are gonna be truly difficult to back out of, look at how your future partner is spending his or her money as your courtship progresses.

For the women: Remember, with many men, money equals status and power. A bit too much money, and he's flinging it around the place like a cartoon version of a Las Vegas slot machine that's been fed methamphetamines instead of quarters. Take note: It says much more about his emotional self than it does about his financial acumen. Here is a guy that may feel a bit inadequate about how he feels about himself. If this continues unabated, you are going to have serious long-term problems.

There is a joke I heard many years ago, about a man and his money. I shouldn't tell it because it's sexist and not gentlemanly. But it certainly illustrates quite clearly a man's attitude towards money, power, status and women.

A man was romantically involved with three women at the same time. He loved them all equally, and he couldn't decide which one to marry. So, he decided to put them all to the test. To each one, he gave a sizeable amount of money to see which one of the three would spend it the most wisely.

When he saw woman number one, he found that she had taken the money he had given her and bought a whole new wardrobe for herself: new gowns, purses and shoes. The whole works. She explained that the new clothes were really for him, as she felt that the better she looked for him, the more desirable he would find her.

Woman number two had done something differently. She had spent half of the money on herself, and the other half on gifts for him, explaining that whatever material possessions she had, or would ever have, would always be shared equally with the man she loved.

Now the third woman took the money and spent it all on him, saying that whatever she had was always his, and that it would always be thus.

So, which woman did he marry?

Wait for it. Wait for it.

The one with the big breasts. Ahem.

If you think about it, it really does illustrate both how men view money and its importance, and how little regard a man may hold it in. More to the point: money is important in a man's life, but he tends to be more reckless with it than women. Just as telling, it also illustrates those different worldviews I spoke of earlier that men and women hold. Men will laugh at this joke while they high-five each other, while most women will dismiss it as "Typical."

Back to business.

Does the man in your life spend money as sparingly as possible on you, himself, or anyone or anything else? Again, this is dangerous ground. Does he charge you interest on the five bucks he lent you? Careful. He's a bit controlling, and you are going to have some problems on your way to driving off that financial cliff.

REAL ADVICE

Should either one of these extremes in his behavior pop up, it probably is the result of the nurture side of him. It could be that he grew up in a family that didn't have many material possessions because of lack of money. Therefore, once he comes into possession of some, he goes a little nuts, or conversely, is so afraid of losing it that he simply can't let go of any.

My Advice? Tame it. Stop it. As soon as the commitment is made, start working on the financial portion of the rest of your life. This could be a bit tricky, so continue to assure him that while you both will be squirreling away most of the combined earned income, he will always have enough to buy a bauble or two.

No matter your marital status, creating a financial plan that takes into account every contingency you both will face months and years down the road (let alone next week) is virtually impossible. In the coming years you will both face unexpected events that will strain if not break your financials: The fire that burned up everything you owned, job(s) lost, the unexpected pregnancy or illness without adequate insurance, the car wreck, cousin Vinny, the mole crickets that ate all your grass, the broken washing machine, and on and on and on.

Whatever your and your soon-to-be mate's current financial picture, and whatever unforeseen events life will dump on you in the years to come, I cannot stress enough the importance of financial planning. It's hard and complex and oftentimes fraught with deadly intentions, but one of you must be completely sane as well as brutally honest.

Ummm, that could very well be you.

First things first, I fully realize that once the whole marriage commitment has been made, wedding planning has now become the hot topic. It's unavoidable, and in its own way, quite fun. But it is by no means the first thing on your one million things to do list. It is number two. Number one is how can we pay down or eliminate any individual debt before our marriage?

It would be so nice if you both owed no one anything, but in today's economy, that ship sailed long ago. Chances are, one or both of you are making payments on student loans, cars, rent, credit cards, and the like. Up until now, your partner's debt was his or hers alone, and like crossing the streams from the Ghostbusters proton packs, mixing them together would cause the destruction of all life on planet Earth. Not a comforting thought.

But now, since you are both taking that great leap forward, some things need to mix and merge, or be gotten rid of. Let's take your current situations first.

My Advice? Pay down as much individual debt as you two possibly can before you get married. That includes the cars (I'm assuming you both own a car), credit cards, student loans, hospital bills that the Goddamned Satanic Insurance Company refused to pay, etc. By the way, I'm a little surprised that there isn't an insurance company by that name. There never will be of course, but you can write Goddamned Satanic Insurance Company in the memo space of the premium check you send to them each month.

You don't need to tell me that paying down your debt(s) can be quite... well... a bitch. It is. But one of you, if not both of you, are carrying some kind of debt. When you were living as singles, it may not have entered the picture. Well, it will now.

REAL ADVICE

For many of you reading this book: if both of you are carrying debt, it may be impossible to get rid of all of it. Student loans can take years to pay off, and who wants to wait to get married until they are 85?

The point is, whittle down as much of it as you can. If you haven't already done so, learn how to operate on a budget and pare down any outpourings of money that you can. In other words, become a responsible adult.

It truly hurt me to say that, but those faceless folks that you owe money to have no sense of decency or humor, and should you fall behind in your payments, they will be right over to collect your car while you are sleeping.

Whether you are successful or not in reducing and/or eliminating some of the debts you owe individually, trying to do so at least gets you two thinking about your financial future, and helps you work together as a team against a common enemy. This represents a pretty good start to married life.

Yay for you.

Now that you are working (somewhat) as a team, you need to start discussing what to do with all that dough you don't have (but know that someday you will). Here is where you start to add the water, two eggs, and vegetable oil and mix until well blended.

Yes, I used that ridiculous metaphor to segue into the joint finance stuff.

My Advice? It may be wise to start out by each of you keeping your own checking accounts and then each contributing to a joint savings account. Please note that even this simple little step can cause great wailing and wringing of hands. Let me explain.

Savings accounts are great. It represents money that both of you don't absolutely need right now, and can sit in some interest bearing account making you both richer by the minute. Not really, but some day...

Anyway, how much each of you contributes is the difficult part. While we are all striving for equality in all phases of life, it's just a matter of fact that sometimes (actually all the time) men and women don't make the same amount of money. He makes more; she makes more. Who puts in what, and when? "If I put in 60%, am I entitled to 60%?" "Bite me."

I am not going to get in the middle of this argument. You two figure it out. But decide to do something with joining your financials. Just remember: We are all human and that means we say and do stupid things. Should push ever come to shove, I don't want to hear about you two yelling at each other about, "You Goddamnedsonofabitch, all this time I have put more money into the savings account than you, so I should get the biggest share. I hate you..."

If you don't work this out, and you do have enough disposable income to put away, all you're left with is getting a checking account in your own name at a bank different than the one you both already have. (Stash your "go" money there.) Yes, the money in there when you get married is legally a joint asset, but it can't be withdrawn by anyone but you. It's safe. And go paperless- you don't need statements or phone calls and such sent to the house do you? Then, get a credit card in your own name on the QT. Use it, pay it off every month (see: checking account) and then you'll be a step ahead of the game should anything bad happen.

My Advice? I know it sounds cool enough, but it's a lie you be tellin'. A lie of omission, but a lie nonetheless. I caution you against this. Do it only if this is your third marriage and your previous spouses had access to all of your money and cleaned house before he or she took off into the night with the hired help (and your car).

Anyway, there's more to do before the marriage besides paying down as much debt as possible, such as planning on a reasonable wedding and honeymoon budget and finding a way to merge your finances.

I speak here of talking with your spouse about goals. Short-term goals. Long-term goals. Plus, maybe something in between.

Goals are important. Everyone should have them. Just be careful here. If your partner wants to someday be the Intergalactic Overlord, maybe you should take away the xBox for the time being.

Short-term goals pertain to such matters as emergency funds for a whole host of things including natural and human disasters, premature graying and mole crickets. Maybe that's something you can afford to do right now, maybe it isn't. That's OK. Just remember, if you do go ahead and set up an emergency fund, you have taken a portion of your money out of circulation, not to be touched until the floodwaters rise. If you can't do it right at this moment, don't, and don't feel bad about it. Do it later. But please do it. After all, sometimes for newlyweds buying Half-and-Half is an emergency.

Obviously, I don't know what your current financial situation is, and I don't presume to council you like you are someone who always has some extra dough floating around. You probably don't. You are probably like the rest of humanity, going from paycheck to paycheck, and secretly dipping into your spouse's purse or wallet just to pay for some precious gasoline. But regardless of your finances, you need to at least consider mid-range goals like buying a house or having a child.

My Advice? Save, save, save. Much, much easier said than done. As I have said many times before: I don't know what your finances are like. Maybe both of your credit scores are solid—maybe not. Maybe you are carrying too much debt at the moment—maybe not. Maybe you have money in savings accounts—maybe not. But remember, the advice I am giving you at the moment is before you get married. So you have time to figure out everything that needs figuring out.

One other piece of advice here: Make sure you are absolutely comfortable discussing the purchase of a house with your prospective mate, but for both of your protection, even if you have the money to put down on a house, it might not be totally wise to buy one before your marriage. Stuff happens. Someone may get left at the altar. Both of you are also (or should be) deeply involved with wedding plans, and it can be virtually impossible to make wise decisions regarding other matters. You can't afford mistakes here. House hunting can truly be an ordeal. House buying can be even worse. Better to hold off until after the marriage. But at least talk with your partner about what you expect in a starter home.

As a personal anecdote, when my wife and I got around to discussing what we wanted in a home, we came to the realization that our visions were much different. I grew up in the north, where most houses had compartmentalized rooms: a living room separated from the family room (rumpus room, den, TV room, whatever) which was separated from the dining room, which was separated from the kitchen, and so on.

She grew up in the south where many of the homes exhibited a more open floor plan. To me, it was a house with one really big room. I couldn't abide essentially eating dinner in the kitchen while looking out at the entire rest of the house. I mean, you can eat lunch in the kitchen, but dinner? Couldn't do it. We had many debates about this. I ducked many a frying pan aimed at my very delicate head. Ultimately, we compromised. Open floor plan, but with a formal dining room. Whew.

Anyway, back to the matter at hand: buying a house. A house is a rather large purchase. In fact, for most people (newlywed or not) it represents the biggest investment you will make in your lifetime. Don't go into it without the proper resources. You may need to have at least 20% of the purchase price to put down on the thing. You have to pay the monthly mortgage, do all of the maintenance yourselves, fix things, paint things, make sure your homeowners insurance is adequate, buy lots and lots of tools and equipment (some you'll use only once), pay property taxes, and of course, kill all of them damn mole crickets in your lawn. So make sure you are both committed. Talk about it. It's bound to be somewhat messy, but you have to get through it. Just make sure you stay loose and limber in case of the flying frying pan whizzing toward your medulla oblongata.

Kind of like having a child, isn't it? Except for the whole mole cricket thing.

And, what a great way to segue into the other rather large mid-term goal: having a child. This whole childbearing thing is actually covered in a future chapter. I am not covering it all here, in part because while important financial considerations need to be made regarding bringing up baby, I'm just not comfortable hashing it all out here on the financial pages. Yes, financials are important when deciding on whether to have a child at a certain point, but I still come down more on the side of emotionality here.

The point is, at least discuss children before you get married. Be totally briefed on what your partner expects on this matter. The last thing you want to happen is to find out that your partner hates children and wants none of it after you are married. By the same token, you don't want to wait until the wedding is over to find out that your spouse wants at least six—three of each. More on this and other matters later.

Long-term goals include investing and retirement. Again, unless you are flush with cash, investment and retirement accounts could be something that you can do after you get back from your honeymoon.

There're lots more things you two need to discuss before the wedding: Who is elected to pay the monthly bills and the day-to-day budget concerns? How much can either of you spend without making it a joint decision? What's our current employment status? Can there actually be a budget for groceries every week? The list is potentially endless, and if you get caught up to your neck in it, then you will both end up hating one another and question every decision you have made up until now. Not a pretty picture.

REAL ADVICE

My Advice? Before you both come face-to face-at the altar and say your, "I dos," talk about it all. Fight about it all. You will live through it. Do what you can when you can do it. Save some of the other details until after all of the dust settles. At least you both are keeping the lines of communication open. And that is a really important step.

Your Finances After Marriage

Assuming you have survived all the prenuptial agony about finances, you should be in better shape than you would be if you two never discussed as many ins and outs as possible. It's also quite possible that both of you were able to come to some decisions about your financials and were able to—at the very least—begin to manage them. Hopefully, you two can now purchase that jar of spicy mustard and the Half-and-Half without getting into another shouting match. All that being said, this second part of the chapter will be much shorter than the first.

Now that you have both discussed (and hopefully done something about) paying down individual debt, pushing up your respective credit scores, discussed the whole bill paying thing, the merging of your finances, the discussions on purchasing a home and having a baby or six (including an ovulation schedule), and were able to get past all of the ego and power matters, all that's left is stuff like living wills, life insurance policies and retirement. Of course, like I always say, "there's more," but these are the big three.

As far as wills go, do one. As far as life insurance policies go, get one. These things are not as sexy as money managers would have you believe, but go a long way to eliminate stress.

Wills can be done rather cheaply and you can do them on the Internet (Think LegalZoom.). Wills are important as they lay out what are called advanced directives that include DNR instructions. Do this as soon as you can just in case that frying pan ever finally reaches its mark and puts you in a coma.

Same thing with life insurance. Do it as soon as possible, again in case of the frying pan scenario. Just remember, life insurance, while relatively inexpensive, means money out of the mainstream of your life. Make sure you can afford what you want before you decide. However, if you find out that your spouse has taken out a million dollar policy on you, and a new shovel shows up in the shed, well, the best thing I can advise you is to duck.

What's left is retirement. I know, you are 40 some years away from that event, but as soon as you can, start putting money away in a retirement account like the Roth IRA cavernous-mouth Suzi and I spoke of earlier. There are many other opportunities for investing in your retirement, but right now a Roth IRA could make sense.

Believe it or not, there is also a Roth 401(k) that works well for some. Instead of the $5,500 yearly limit the Roth IRA has, the Roth 401(k) allows you to put in up to $16,500 each year. I'll wait for all of your laughter to stop. Yes, you probably don't have that kind of money laying around in a duffel bag somewhere in the attic, but the operative phrase here is, "up to." You don't have to put in that much, but you can go up to it. Both offer a lot of the same bennies, but personally, I like the tax benefits of the Roth IRA.

A big caveat here. Drawing out your money early on the Roth plans gives you a penalty (10%). So before you even think about getting whatever vehicle to build your nest egg on, have an emergency fund. I should put that in bold type, but just let me repeat it: have an emergency fund. Why, you ask? Because if you don't have such a fund and a real honest-to-God emergency arises, then you will have to dip into the Roth for some ready cash and quite possibly destroy all the sacrifices you have made to ensure your happiness in retirement. As I said, being a responsible adult is a bit of a bitch, isn't it?

There are also the "regular" 401(k)s. Many times the company you work for offers one of these retirement vehicles. Your company and you are both contributors to this fund, so your money can grow relatively fast.

For those of you who are not familiar with this retirement fund, a 401(k) plan is the common name in the USA for a tax-qualified, defined-contribution, pension account. Under the plan, retirement savings contributions are provided (and sometimes proportionately matched) by your employer. Money is deducted from your paycheck before taxation, (therefore deferring any taxes until you withdraw it during your retirement). Limits are a lot higher than the Roth IRA, and you and your employer can contribute a maximum pre-tax annual amount of about $18,000 each year. This could mean that if you stay with the same company year after miserable year, you could have contributed well over half a million dollars. Add your spouse's savings into the mix and riding horses on that beach is not so much of a wild fantasy anymore.

Of course, all this assumes that your employer remain solvent enough to continue making said contributions, or doesn't close its doors created by a sudden downturn in the economy. Just remember the year 2008 when millions of folks lost all of their 401(k) money and were left with nothing for retirement. You can tell who they are just by walking into your local Wal-Mart store.

There are many rules and restrictions (and taxes) with these 401(k)s, (you can even borrow on them should the need arise.), so vet it fully before you commit.

My Advice? When making a valiant attempt at putting money aside for the future, whether short-term, long-term and/or anything in between, make sure you don't get locked in. It is important that you stay as liquid as possible. It's always nice to start that college funds for your designer clone babies, but a sudden job loss could wipe out your emergency fund and then some, and there you go, dipping into that Harvard college fund to pay the mortgage. It may be your only option when it comes due.

Another personal anecdote. I'm not proud of it, but I used to swear-a lot. I was the champion of swearing, weaving an intricate tapestry of invectives all around the house. When my children were young, but had the power of speech and understanding, they made me donate money to a swear jar whenever I, shall we say, misspoke. In a very short time we had enough to take all four of the children for a holiday weekend at Disney World.

I don't curse much any more. I miss it, but the alternative would be to spend much time at Fantasy Island with the family. I mean, I love them all, but four little girls? It can be brutal. But at least I had ready access to some dough. Someday you may find this out for yourself.

The important thing here is always make sure you have easy and quick access to any money you have been able to put away.

REAL ADVICE

Look, chances are, your life together will be one of happiness and mutual satisfaction. This will always be true if neither one of you ever ventures outside of the house or accepts incoming phone calls and mail delivery. Money has a tendency to complicate matters, especially the lack of it.

My Advice? In dealing with your present financial picture, only do what you can at the time you need to do it. No fudging or making promises you can't keep. Be willing to admit that, "Right now, we're tapped out. I/we will keep it in mind, but for right now, we can't make it happen."

I know that at some time in your marriage, one of you is going to lie about how much something costs, or how much money you both have stuffed under the mattress, or, "Yes I paid that last week." And I also know that you will fight over your finances. It's gonna happen. Stay steady and weather whatever storm is brewing. You need to do this simply because through your years together, you will have many more of the stupidest fights you can imagine.

I speak of the in-laws.

Chapter Seven

Ya Know, I Really Hate Your Parents

or

Ya Know, I Think Your Parents Really Hate Me

Ahhh, the "other" parentals (your parents, of course, are pretty much just fine. It's your partner's parents that are just killing you.). Regardless as to whom they belong to, they all come in so many different shapes, sizes and personality quirks, don't they? They come from the widest variety of life experiences and prejudices and go from the inane to the insane. Parents. Can't say enough about them. (Well, actually I am about to.)

But the parentals, no matter how they come at you, and rest assured they will, have one thing in common: "Look, we've gone through this when we got married. We know what we're talking about. Now put on that second wedding gown you tried on before, you know, the one with those pretty pink roses sewn onto the bodice. The one that makes you look all bumpy and fat. I just love it. And I know you will too. You know I'm right."

You may not think parents play that big of a role in things after you turn 16, but wait until you decide to get married. "When your mother and I got married, we..."

Regardless of whether your parents can be described as the helicopter types or the laissez faire types, or anything in between, if you thought they (both your partner's and yours) were a pain in the ass while you two were dating, they can be even worse after you have made the decision to wed.

There are many combinations to these interpersonal and complex relationships: how the boyfriend sees the girlfriend's mom, how he sees the girlfriend's dad, how he sees them as parental units, how he sees his girlfriend when she is with them, how he sees their influence on her when she is not with them, blah, blah, blah. The same holds true for the girl and his parents.

Of course, parents being parents and full of all that life experience stuff they try to impart to you on a minute-by-minute schedule, they pretty much disapprove of just about everything you do: "When your mother and I got married, we..."

There's a lot of nurture stuff happening here, and it's complicated. Often, too much so. And whether you both get through it depends pretty much on where your pressure points are and whether you are resilient enough to emotional pain. If you cried when Bambi died, then I suggest you put off meeting the parents until you are much tougher and wiser.

There are those lucky couples though, who for one reason or another, never have a problem with the future in-laws, or problems once those future in-laws become de jure ones. It's very rare, like seeing Congress agree on some piece of legislation, or Simon Cowell being humble, but it does happen.

And I am sorry, but I will not be able to give you any real advice on making this "liking" part happen for you. Regardless of any advice I would give, I know the truth only too well: Either the parents are going to like you, or they won't-no matter what you do. Just keep in mind that these interpersonal interplays can be quite complicated, and if not managed correctly, can destroy self-esteems, relationships and entire planets like nothing else.

Sorry, it's just a fact.

The Parentals Before Marriage

First, let's take a look at the parents before marriage. So as to create as much confusion as possible, I will be jumping back and forth between both sexes as well as the moms and dads.

From the male perspective, it can be much worse than from the female perspective. When the young man finally meets the parents, it's almost always at their house, which is totally unfair because they have the home field advantage. That's always worth three points. But when you're young, a free meal is a free meal.

REAL ADVICE

Once again, let me interject a caveat here. It is the 21st century, but some things still ring true. What follows may not represent your experience with getting everyone together to size each other up. Also, for the most part, moms and dads are different these days, but often times they fall back on the way they were treated by their partner's parents when they were first dating (which usually was pretty brutal). Your venture, as you wade into this potential hellhole, may actually be quite enjoyable.

No, probably not.

Back to the free meal thing. Mom will probably be quite cordial as she invites you into the family domicile. She will be gracious and warm. She will do all she can to smooth out any edginess you may have about this encounter.

"Good evening Mrs. (insert mom's last name here). It's so nice to finally meet you." "Oh please," she answers, "Call me Martha."

Beware, boys. She is what is known as the Judas goat. A Judas goat is a trained goat used in animal herding. The Judas goat is used to hang out with sheep or cattle, and has been trained to lead them to a specific destination. In stockyards, a Judas goat will lead those sheep or cattle to slaughter, while its own life is spared.

Ladies of mothers, I mean this in the nicest possible way.

"Just whom is to be slaughtered?" you ask. Well, you young man, you. "And just who will be doing the slaughtering?" Well, dad, young man, dad. He's the one walking out of the bathroom just as you sit down on the comfortable, soft couch all prepared nice, nice by mom. He may have a sharp, pointy tool in his hand, or maybe just the crossword page from the evening paper. He may ultimately stab you with the sharp pointy thing, or ask you, "What's a nine letter word for the brutal slaying of a person? (It's slaughter, by the way) Either way, you are screwed.

You jump up off of the couch and you lamely say, "Good evening Mr. (insert pop's last name here). I'm very glad to meet you." "Oh, please," he answers. "Just call me Colonel."

You stick out your hand for him to shake.

Several possibilities will happen here. Either you will swing and miss on this handshake thing, only inserting your fingers into the palm of his hand, thereby getting them crushed and this all makes you feel like a sissy boy. Even if you get it right, he will grab your hand very firmly and squeeze really hard, daring you to not wince. Another possible scenario is that dad pretends not to see your shaking, outstretched hand and simply decides not to acknowledge it, all the while taking bets with himself as to how long you're going to stand there looking for all the world like a dumb ass while he plants himself in the chair directly in front of you.

One last possibility involves him cordially responding to your outstretched hand with an outstretched hand of his own and gently, but firmly takes your hand into his, replete with a warm and friendly smile. His left hand also comes lightly down upon both of your hands, making it a two fisted handshake. You both clasp on another in a loving hand embrace as your arms move up and down twice, maybe thrice, and he graciously invites you to retake your seat in the soft comfy couch lovingly prepared all nice, nice by mom.

REAL ADVICE

No, probably not.

Regardless of the greeting you receive from daddy, the entire evening is designed to intimidate you and gather as much information from you as possible in about two of the longest hours you will ever spend in your young life. I include the PSATs here to give you a better idea.

Fathers and boyfriends are natural enemies. Think mongoose and cobra; lion and zebra; the assassin bug and the grasshopper. This last one is quite apt. All assassin bugs are predators; some species feed on insects while others feed on the blood of mammals. And that's daddy. Either he's going to eat the young man up or exsanguinate him before the night is through. And no matter how high up one thinks one is on the food chain, fathers trump it.

Boys you must remember this: Through all of the grilling, the feigned laughter and the knowing looks, sitting in front of you is the Grand Inquisitor. For in his head, daddy knows you are lying like hell just to get on his good side and into his daughter's pants.

"Oh yes sir, I plan on going to college and becoming an architect, where I will design a collection of energy efficient, affordable homes for those less fortunate. Of course, that's after a stint in the Peace Corps where I will help eliminate hunger and disease. Then I plan on spending time as a volunteer at Walter Reed Hospital, helping out with the Wounded Warrior program. I'm just hoping that it will not interfere with my acolyte duties at my churches vespers, or with my volunteering at the local soup kitchen."

Bullshit, bullshit, bullshit.

Every time you say something, anything, only two things are going on in dad's head: One is bullshit, bullshit, bullshit. The second is, "I used to be you, kid. I would say anything to my wife's parents as long as I could get into their daughter's pants about 15 minutes after we headed out of there. And as sure as I know there is a God in heaven, all you want to do is touch my Little Angel's dirty places. I'll kill you."

My Advice? Remember, because of the long standing tradition of the girl's parents meeting the boyfriend, and the mess of trouble that can spring from it, what I say here probably won't make them like you more, but it may help you from the standpoint that they also won't hate you more.

First, look dad straight in the eye. Be careful with this however. According to those who study the art of body language and animal husbandry, looking at a person too long or intently can be an act of power and domination. Looking down involves not looking at the other person, which may be a sign of submission: "I am not a threat, really; please do not hurt me. You are so glorious the light of your radiance would blind me if I gazed too long at you. You are the sun from which all power and resplendency flows, and all of us just revolve around you and your magnificence." So look at him, but don't stare too much.

Don't mumble. Don't get roped into political NeoCon conversations or "Why the hell does the Pope wear that stupid hat?" conversations. No religion if you can help it. Sports talk is cool, but do not (even if it's true) let on that you may know more about current sport topics than dad does (it's a male ego thing). Just give him enough info so that he knows you are not that sissy boy who messed up during the handshake.

REAL ADVICE

My Advice? Remain calm and stay true to your real self. If dad punctuates his sentences with a wide variety of swear words, do not take this as your cue to join in—it's a trap—do not swear. Do not share any intimate details of private moments you may have had with his daughter. Remember the sharp pointy thing he may have come out of the bathroom with? He will now use it on you. Chew your dinner with your mouth closed. Compliment mom on the wonderfully prepared haggis, and certainly let her know that the raw asparagus spears were a nice touch. If offered an alcoholic drink, do not accept. Tell dad that your throat is really dry and you would prefer something sweet at the moment, perhaps a coke. The drink thing is also a trap. Is he a drinker? Will he loosen his tongue after one or two scotches? Under no circumstances should you imbibe with daddy on your first date with him. Maybe next time, but not now.

If dad mentions that he is working on some kind of "special" project—whether it is home improvements or something that has to do with dynamite—do not quickly volunteer your help. This is a sure sign to pops that you are just showing off or sucking up, and he will want no part of it. Besides, he doesn't know you. You are not one of his friends. To a man, these "special" projects are just that— special, and not everyone gets to participate. It is quite possible that being a smart ass college boy, you will probably mentioned that whatever he's doing could be done differently. You also need to consider that you have absolutely zero knowledge of, and therefore no understanding of, what he is doing. Should you try and help him, you will only add more proof to the dumb ass thing he already thinks you are. Better to wait a few days after carefully considering your options, then call to see if he needs any help. The few days wait can really help. Trust me on this.

116

Take as many cues from your girl as you can regarding table manners. Be attentive to her, but under no circumstances, kiss her or even hug her. Don't look at her breasts, and for God sakes, don't size up mom.

There are entire categories regarding this first meeting that I have not touched on. But if you can at least smile, no matter what is done or said, stay sober, not get all of the blood drained from your body, you will come out better for it and with your sac intact.

So dinner is over and you have said your goodbyes. After checking all of your body parts and wiping all of the flop sweat from your brow, you will find that you are still intact and your girl still loves you (maybe). But remember, just because you have left your girl's parents, doesn't mean that they will clear the table and relax in front of the TV. (By the way, you should have helped clean the table after dinner without being asked or even verbalizing anything about it. Just do it real casual-like. Dumb ass.) They will talk about you. They will have somehow managed to get your Social Security Number. They will begin to Google your Facebook page, your Instagram and Twitter accounts. They will track your movements via your cell-phone activity. They will Google your parent's Facebook page. In fact, every day from hereon in, they will talk about you. So your first visit with them better be real good.

Don't take this personally, but they will probably hate you, and when asked later by the daughter what their thoughts are concerning you, they will lie and say that, "He seems like a nice young man." Later, after months of the courtship, the truth will finally come out: "We had hoped that you would have aimed a bit higher."

REAL ADVICE

Now for young ladies who are brought over to the young man's house to meet the parents, things are a bit more refined and in contrast, rather subdued. There is still the warm greeting from mom who wants none of the "Good evening, Mrs. (insert mom's last name here)." "You simply must call me (insert mom's first name here)." Mom is not playing the Judas Goat roll in this evenings production. She is cast as Almira Gulch (The Wicked Witch of the North in the Wizard of Oz.). She's the one with the iron fist hidden by the velvet glove she is wearing. And she's the one our little Dorothy needs to keep focused on.

While dads generally execute a frontal assault on the young man during his first visit, moms often times will come from the flanks—not head on. This is called passive aggression.

In the simplest of terms, passive aggression is really a defense mechanism. It allows people who aren't comfortable being openly aggressive get what they want under the facade of still trying to please others. They want their way, but they also want everyone to still like them. Passive-aggression can be frustrating to its target as well. Being so subtle, it is almost imperceptible since it's not always easily identifiable—or unacceptable—as, say, hooking up electrodes to your sensitive parts and firing up the generator. And mothers are the masters at this.

One hint that she's showing these tendencies is that all evening she continually calls you by your first name. It's Janet this and Janet that. "And wouldn't it be so nice, Janet, if..."

Too bad your name is Janice.

Virtually every question she asks you or every statement she makes will, like a fine wine, have passive-aggressive notes.

For example, she may hit you right off with the, "My son has told us so much about you. I feel as though I really know you. Let me say that you seem to be doing just fine for someone with your background and education."

Another scenario may play itself out thusly: "I'm sorry," the young woman says to mom. "But we were in a hurry to get here, and I just didn't have enough time to get ready. I hope I'm not too underdressed." "Think nothing of it, my dear. Besides, maybe just five more pounds and your outfit will look really good on you."

Huh?

She may also whisper into your ear something directed at junior, such as: "Oh my goodness, he was such a little darling when he was growing up, except for all those tantrums."

Answering any of these passive-aggressive questions and statements will produce a mixed bag, and depending on the mom, you may endear yourself with a snappy comeback or just a simple smile. In any event do not, under any circumstances, run out of the kitchen sobbing with your hands covering your face. Not being able to see clearly, and not knowing the layout of the house, you may bump into something and hurt yourself—or worse, run into some fragile family heirloom and bust it up real good.

The young man's father on the other hand really doesn't care too much. As long as the young lady has nice hair, ample breasts, all of her teeth and shows no signs of heroin addiction, he's pretty well set. Besides, "Finally, my boy's getting laid."

REAL ADVICE

My Advice? As soon as you take off your coat or jacket, tell mom how wonderful the house looks, and, "Oh my, what smells so good?" Offer to lend a hand in the kitchen. If politely rebuffed on this, tell her you are no stranger to kitchen work and it would be an absolute honor and a pleasure to humbly assist her in her endeavors. Just like what may have happened to your young man at your house, don't acquiesce to the alcoholic drink thing. You may need to somehow reassure mom that no, you are not refusing to have any alcohol because you are pregnant. You just don't drink, ever.

Again, I know that as human beings we have been evolving at a rapid pace. Men cook and do the laundry; women are quite capable at using power tools and lawn mowing—just not tonight. Tonight, mom is June Cleaver, and dad is Ward (on steroids). And June has spent the better part of 18 years feeding and picking up after little junior and getting to know you will go a long way to assuaging any trepidation she has concerning who her little boy is hooking up with.

Unlike my previous advice to the young man, do not take as many cues from your boy as you can regarding table manners. Correct him as necessary; quietly and efficiently. By doing this, you are sending a subtle but non-threatening message to mom that you are quite capable of picking up the care and feeding of little junior where she left off.

Be attentive to him, but under no circumstances, let him kiss you or even hug you. Don't look at his junk, but it is OK to size up daddy—once. It will feed his ego a bit, for after about twenty years of marriage, wifey no longer looks at his junk and pretty much regards him as a muley with a paycheck. Careful on this however, don't feed his ego or laugh too hard at his off-color jokes. Mom will take offense at this and do something passive-aggressive—like spitting in your coffee.

Speaking of laughter, if you've got one of those laughs, you know, the one where you snort at the end? Or the one where your laughter sounds like a machine gun? Practice not doing this before you arrive. I have always found it amazing how many quality people have been crossed off my list based on a goofy laugh. "She seemed like a really sweet girl, and very pretty. But that laugh. Did you ever...?"

Again, everything can go exactly as planned and a warm friendly gathering ensues. Mom gets along with the girlfriend while dad grudgingly accepts the young man. While under constant pressure to perform, a fine meal is eaten along with light, but meaningful conversation. In short, everyone involved has had a great time. Promises are made to do it again real soon.

No, probably not.

Chances are, somebody burped or farted. Somebody snorted at the end of their laugh. Somebody choked on the haggis. Somebody said something stupid. Somebody did something stupid. Somebody did not have a good time.

Now before we leave this part and go on to the next, remember way back in Chapter Five when I told you to look for "tells?" Those tells come in real handy here. Watch how your boy interacts with his parents. Watch how your girl interacts with hers.

Each of you, when left to your own devices and are operating apart from the rents, will exhibit at least a modicum of independent thoughts and actions. But surround him or her with the parents and you may find a completely different person than the one you have fallen in love with.

Is she still daddy's little angel who hangs on to his every word? Is she a momma clone who exhibits that same passive-aggressive side? Does he accept the verbal abuse and idiotic career/financial advice from dad? Does he act like he's 6-years-old when he's around mom?

These little tells can be so revealing. Watch for them carefully. Pay attention to them. They could forecast future behavior that you will have to deal with for the next 50 or so years.

My Advice? Regardless of how the evening went, you both now need to go out and get a stiff drink, followed by some nice sex. You need to decompress. Talk to each other about how you think the evening went. Talk about your impressions and how you felt when his mom told you not to worry: "I'm sure your face will clear up, and your makeup at least hides most of the worst of it." Tell your girlfriend that the sharp pointy thing daddy was holding may have "accidentally" severed one of your main arteries and to please drop me off at the nearest hospital. You both need some time to relieve yourselves from the seriousness of the evening.

Stay long enough at the bar and have enough alcohol so you can both start laughing about what transpired a short time ago. But be careful. Don't start ragging on his or her parents. Always bear in mind that your partner can make fun of his or her parents, but you can't. No need to start a fight now.

Also, remember to leave the bar as soon as you both are more relaxed and are able to joke about things. You are going to have sex now, and you need to at least be a little bit coherent.

Well, you have both weathered the storm and through the ensuing months or years, relations with each others parents have gotten a bit better and more cordial on subsequent interactions. Now that you two have decided on this marriage thing, everything may change.

Bonus Section!

Doesn't everybody love getting a free drink with their hamburger and fries? This section is sort of like that. Instead of just two sections like in the previous chapters, in this one there are three.

We should all feel good about this.

I know I do.

The Transition

(Not yours, but the transition from the parentals just being the parentals, to them becoming the future in-laws.)

That's a pretty long title, I know, but I'm just not going to apologize for it.

Even though most newly married couples wish that in-laws sometimes didn't come as a package deal, it just isn't so. Wouldn't it be nice to only accept the money both sets of parents are willing to throw at all of the wedding expenses, and leave all the relationship-building to someone much more qualified?

Maybe Dr. Phil.

REAL ADVICE

I'm sorry to break the news to you, but that ain't gonna happen. In-laws come into your lives whether it is a good thing or a bad thing. When you marry another person, you not only wed him or her, you marry a family. Correction—you marry the whole damned family. This includes not only Martha and the Colonel, but crazy uncle Fred and his wife, Dolores. You marry cousin Vinnie and all four of his buck-toothed offspring. You marry your partner's brother or sister. You marry everyone.

And, not only will you have to spend holidays with all of these people, but they will all come to the wedding. Martha and the Colonel will see to that.

That is not to say that the future in-laws are a collection of assho... well actually they are. And the sad thing is, each one of you will have to fit into each other's families. They will not change for you. You change for them (at least in the short term). It's an accommodation you will have to make for all of ten minutes. After that, you really will want to run out of the room with your hands covering your face and not care whether you run into some precious family heirloom and bust it all to hell and back.

Obviously, the transition time I speak of is called the wedding. And in-law intrusions into this realm are unavoidable. In all probability, the pre-wedding rituals such as dress buying, guest lists, attendants, food tasting (along with the ever popular alcohol tasting), the DJ hiring (please dear God, not cousin Vinny), and the like, will be the peak time for tensions to come to the forefront.

I can only stress to both of you on the need to be careful here. Through your long (or short) courtship, you have probably been saving up some really good comebacks you have stored in your head to all of the personal slights and passive-aggressive behaviors aimed at all of your sensibilities. Going over old ground and pointing fingers will only lead to complete and total disarray and possibly ruin what might otherwise be an enjoyable day.

For many engaged couples, interference in the wedding plans by a family member being poopy from either side, can be a major source of hostility and only earn poopiness back from you (This is what your mom used to call "tit for tat.").

By the way, all of us have used the phrase, "tit for tat." As a young boy, I always found it sounded a bit dirty, you know, "tit." Well, even though most of the world knows that it means retribution or retaliation, did you know that it comes from the Olde English words "tip" and "tap?" Well it does. Tip and tap originally meant small blows or hits. Over the years it has been modified into tit and tat. Who knows why, but now at least you know where the hell all these little sayings originated from.

And did you also know that there is another little ditty that almost no one knows: "Tit for two tats." Tit for two tats, while very similar to tit for tat, it is much nicer, forgiving and does not include much, if any, screaming and shouting. The difference between the two is how forgiving this strategy is.

See how much new and stupid information you can find when you're really not even looking?

My Advice? Since I am the one giving advice here, might I suggest the latter as the strategy you probably should use? That's the one where you do metaphorically hit back, but you are smiling.

REAL ADVICE

These little power battles from your about-to-be extended family members have the capacity to spew noxious venom all over anything and everything, causing deep, slashing wounds that may ultimately poison the in-law/extended family relationship forever. This is supposed to be a time of great celebration and enormous joy for all concerned. But domineering and bad behaviors can cause all kinds of problems that are sometimes much too hard and complex for either of you to handle effectively.

I hate to say this, but both sides are often guilty of being insensitive to both sets of the, "others" and their almost fanatical desire to help. This is because each of you think that this is, "Your Special Day," and both of you can be a bit judgmental, as well as ungrateful and selfish.

Feel Better?

Not to make you feel any worse, but the hard cold truth is: This is not "Your Special Day."

All those magazine articles you've been reading and all those daydreams that you've been having about your wedding day are pretty much wrong. And don't you just hate that, because you and your intended have sat around together, planning and planning this thing for months. You've purchased your fair share of bridal magazines and cut out the appropriate photos. You've Googled about 250 wedding websites looking for advice and "How To's." You've themed the whole damned thing down to the species of rose petals that are to be thrown on the aisle. You've Facebooked about it. You've Tweeted about it.

It's at this point when all of the preliminary stuff is done, that both of you now see it. You can visualize it. You picture everything. You see it in your respective dreams. It's perfect.

Ahh crap. You informed the parents, didn't you. Damn.

So before you purchase your fair share of bridal magazines and cut out the appropriate photos. Before you Google about 250 wedding websites looking for advice and "How To's." Before you theme the whole damned thing down to the species of rose petals that are to be thrown on the aisle. Before you Facebook about it. Before you Tweet about it—read this part of the book like your life depends on it. It does—at least the healthy part of it.

Please don't misunderstand me when I say this, but weddings, like funerals are community events. The wedding day is not really as private as you were led to believe. In fact, it's a myth. We hold societal ceremonies like weddings and funerals to affirm a life (or in your case, lives). They must therefore be communal. Marriages (and funerals) affirm what a person(s) have done with their lives, or are about to do. For all the blows it has taken, traditional marriage ceremonies, replete with extended family-type people are institutions ingrained in virtually all cultures living on this planet. Marriage, witnessed by all of the bride's "community" as well as the groom's "community," gives it a true sense of moral and legal legitimacy. "Oh hell yeah. They's hitched alright. We all done gone and witnessed it all. Hell of a reception, too. Heh, heh."

Consider yourself lucky: In South Korea they have a tradition of beating the grooms feet with a fish—a Goddamned fish. All the while they throw questions at him that he must answer. All this is supposed to make him stronger and more knowledgeable for the wedding evening. This is a great tradition, but really, what bride wants to hop into bed with a man who smells like a dead fish—a Goddamned fish.

Among the Tidong who live in Northern Borneo (I'll wait till you get done Googling where the hell Borneo is), newlyweds aren't allowed to go to the bathroom for three days after the wedding. They can shower and stuff, but no urinating, and no bowel movements—for three Goddamned days—*three*. Why, you ask? As I understand it, if you can get through 72 full hours of this torture, your marriage will pretty much survive anything. It would bring bad luck not to do so. They are so serious about this whole ritual that members of the extended family (the in-law thing again) will actually stand guard at the couple's bathroom door, preventing the newlyweds to do what comes natural for three days. Damn.

Lastly, while American brides totally worry and fret (sometimes obsessively so), over their bridal weight, in certain parts of Northwest Africa, young girls are sent to "fat farms" to actually put on weight in anticipation of their wedding day. They have been known to eat up between 15,000 to 20,000 calories each day. Like the Tidongs, they are so serious about this fattening up that girls can be beaten for refusing food. Again, why you ask? Just like many of the ancients, obesity is a sign of opulence and riches, and an obese bride allows the groom to flaunt his status. Man, 20,0000 calories a day-that's a lot of Little Debbies.

Here in America, brides and grooms pretty much just worry about getting through the ceremony intact: dancin' and drinkin' at the reception, collecting envelopes stuffed with cash, and skating away for a few days.

All this is great. Having all the extended families in attendance is what makes weddings such wonderful occasions; two families and their friends, and their friend's friends coming together to celebrate a lifetime commitment of two of their own.

But while we're all here, let's talk briefly about one of your outs—elopement. Yes, that elopement. And no, the young man doesn't really bring a ladder over to her house and have her climb down it, jump into his hot rod, and run away to Vegas on a full tank of gas and 20 bucks in his wallet. But it's close because it's done in secret.

In its simplest form, eloping just means that the young couple, fraught with incredible pressure from the extended families, see absolutely no way to make or keep anyone happy (let alone themselves). So, they gather up a few trusted friends as well as a select group of family members, and quietly go get hitched.

Utterly at your wits end and completely overwhelmed by time, extended family relationships and money needed to plan a big wedding, who could really blame you? And being honest, during all of the craziness wedding planning can cause, I am absolutely sure that one if not both of you at least considered the elopement thing.

Empirically, there are no fast and firm statistics on different types of marriages in America, including eloping. But a case can be made to at least anecdotally say that eloping is becoming an increasingly attractive option for some couples.

As I mentioned way back in the beginning of this book, many more couples are living together and doing it longer and even having families without the marriage label. When those couples ultimately do decide to marry, elopement can be easier and cheaper.

Why elope, you ask? Simple: money (not enough), time (even less), stress (way too much), and shifting attitudes (a pretty good rationale).

Just think about it for a moment. There truly can be a whole bunch of benefits from a smaller, less formal wedding.

First is the money involved in the wedding you may be currently planning.

Remember what I said in Chapter One? The average cost of a wedding in America has grown in leaps and bounds. A wedding now may cost up to $20,000. Really, if the parentals and the future in-laws don't pony up, who's got $20,000 lying around somewhere? Better to take that money (if you have it or can get your hands on it) and put it down on a perfectly good starter home.

Leaving behind the money end of things, societal changes are eroding the stigma that used to be associated with elopement. Back in the day, you could hear the whispers: "You remember the Johnson kid? Well I heard last week that she and that no-good boyfriend of hers ran away and got married in the next town over. I wouldn't be surprised if the next time we see them, she'll have a 'little one' in tow, if you know what I mean. Poor Martha and the Colonel. They must be beside themselves. Thank God my little Julia is as ugly as she is, so I don't think I'll ever have that problem."

Because we are not back in the day, there exist more situations that compound things even further and add more justification for eloping. More families are additionally complicated today because of the fact that divorce has become less stigmatized. Chances are one of you may have multiple sets of in-laws, step-brothers and/or sisters, buck-toothed second cousins twice removed and other extended family members. And if you are really unlucky, both of you might have two sets of parents—that equals four in-laws. If this is the case, you have my blessing on the elopement thing. If you do end up in this mess, you will spend at least three full days arguing over just who sits where. There is not enough scotch in the world to fix this.

My Advice? I say this without fear of any and all legal reprisals: Trust me. Elope.

However, if you've both decided that at the end of all this madness, you really do want as many family members at your wedding that your budget will allow, you both decide to vote no on the elopement idea. Besides, getting married at the Billy Idol "White Wedding Chapel" with Agnes and her preacher husband, Zeb who got his hitchin' license from the Original Intergalactic Church of Barbecue and Coleslaw, just doesn't seem all that magical.

We are now back to: "This is not your day." And since you have decided to include family and extended family members (including all those with buck teeth), you must now read the book entitled, *The Art of War* by Sun Tzu. This is a book composed of 13 chapters, each one laying out military tactics and strategies for nations at war with each other. Pick the appropriate chapter and operate accordingly.

Of course, before you go nuclear because of all the demands on you, remember: even Sun Tzu, the most famous of military tacticians and strategists said: "The war should be fought swiftly to avoid economic losses: No long war ever profited any country: 100 victories in 100 battles is simply ridiculous. Anyone who excels in defeating his enemies triumphs before his enemy's threats become real".

According to the book, one must avoid massacres and atrocities because this can provoke resistance and possibly allow an enemy to turn the war in his favor. For the victor, "The best policy is to capture the state intact; it should be destroyed only if no other options are available".

My Advice? Be as gracious and as appreciative to the future in-laws and fellow travelers as possible. Try not to use the nuclear option. Almost everyone involved will attempt to give you guidance in the form of unasked for advice. Thank them. Let them know that you cherish every little piece of unsolicited advice they have given you. Tell them you are ever so happy that they are playing such a prominent role in your life.

Ahh, yes, grasshopper, making these little compromises and exceptions at this juncture helps prepare you both for future events such as having babies and letting them completely decide what you do, and when, and how you do it.

In order for this in-law transition time to go as smoothly as possible, you must, at all costs, present a strong and united front with your fiancé. Jabbering some long-held resentment towards your future in-law(s) at the food tasting table without letting your betrothed in on the joke beforehand can be a real killer.

Of course, human beings being what they are, it's not always easy to be on the same page with each other. And here is where it can get a bit tricky. It has long been assumed (and pretty much true) that the future groom really, really hates all of this wedding planning stuff. It's not that he totally hates it; it's just that he will normally reach his saturation point long before the future bride does.

Therefore, from time-to-time (if not pretty much always) he will turn a deaf ear to all of the ideas and suggestions the future bride will make. He figures that all he has to do is round up a bunch of his buddies from The Shamrock Bar and Grill and have them get tuxes, get one of his own, make sure the DJ has been hired, order all of those designer craft beers he is in love with and then show up on the actual day of the wedding, and on time. Remember the road map analogy I mentioned earlier.

One of you needs to make rock sure that you are both operating from the same playbook. It is imperative that concerning the entire spectrum of the wedding planning you both are in agreement on everything, from the lighting in the chapel as well as the dance floor at the reception venue, to the specific species of rose petals to be strewn down the aisle, and to the brand and type of whiskey you will all be drinking. This united front may be something out of Sun Tzu's book, but in order to win the day, I strongly urge you to do this.

As we navigate through our lives, we all have had someone turn on us: our friends, our coworkers, hell, even our pet gerbil. Now that you two have decided to get married, someone will turn on you.

Discounting one of the bride's maids who stomps out over the lime-green taffeta gown she has to wear, and the other folks who hate you because the seating arrangements aren't to their liking, and the third cousin twice removed who wasn't invited, usually that just leaves the in-laws who now may be turning on you.

No matter how complacent and seemingly docile the future in-laws seem to have been while you were dating—just suggest a marriage to them. All of a sudden they go native on you. You will now see first hand examples of the words "critical," "disgruntled," "controlling" and "irrational." Every decision you make is open to examination and criticism. If you go left, you should have gone right. If go right, you should have gone left. If you go up, you should have gone down. If you go down, you should have gone up.

Where in the hell does all this acrimony come from? Let's take a look.

Sometimes we all have to think outside ourselves (you know, that critical thinking/reflecting crap you learned in Philosophy 101). We have to ask ourselves, "How does he feel about what I'm saying? Why is she doing what she's doing? How come he never...?"

It is that inner voice you need to be listening to right now. When you were tiny, the parentals (hopefully) took care of all your wants and needs. They were the ones who took out that college fund for you ten minutes after your birth. Of course, they also were the ones who cashed it in two years later to buy the mini van they had to carry you around in whenever you had colic. Every night while your mom breastfed you at 3 am, she and pops talked about all the possibilities of your life. They had you being a great athlete, the prom king or queen, your high-school student body president, saving a batch of puppies from a fire, attending Harvard on a full ride, becoming president of the United States and marrying the perfect person. Perfect.

Well, when you hit your teens, daddy's little princess or little bandit, started drifting away and you lost your emotional touch with each other. You felt you needed to form opinions and beliefs that were uniquely your own. You began to dabble in Eastern Philosophy. You sang with the Emo band. You saved a whale. You got lots and lots of beads at Mardi Gras. This initial foray by you into your own private world broke mommy's and daddy's collective hearts. "Our child is kind of getting away from us."

With the exception of you needing some dough from time-to-time, or a safe place to crash, you felt pretty much independent of your parents.

Now you've told them that you want to get married.

"Holy shit," says the Colonel. "You're not pregnant, are you?" "It was the breastfeeding that made all the difference," says Martha.

However, as they look at your impending marriage, they are now back in your life in a big way, and trust me, they really don't want to muck things up.

But they probably will.

Each set of parents will end up competing with the other set of parents to see who can do the coolest thing, or spend the most money or capture the bride and groom's ear on all of the issues at hand.

My Advice? Let them. They feel better for it, and the more they compete, the more stuff you'll get. Of course, you and your fiancé will need to get a handle on all of this madness before you guys go crazy and blood starts spurting out of your ears.

REAL ADVICE

But there is so much more.

While you and your fiancé have jumped on the carnival roller coaster (not the one where you go up and down, but the one where you go up and down and inside out and end-over-end. The one that ends with you throwing up all over the place.) Your parents have jumped on one of their own. This is where that Philosophy 101 course on critical thinking/reflecting can pay off.

Try to remember that while you are experiencing a mountain of emotions and pressure to do this thing correctly, the parents are going through their own version.

We've already gone through the competition thing, but there are other forces at work here.

I speak firstly of a sense of loss. Of course they are all happy for you both. But as rebellious as you might have been as a teenager in high school, and as much as they paced the floor hoping you wore clean underwear in case of the car accident you were surely to have, they still knew that eventually you would come home (just about) every night.

Then, when you went away to college, in order to stay in touch with you, they learned how to email and Skype. This probably took some doing:

Mom: "I keep getting an error message when I try to print out the documents you sent me on the interweb."

Child: "Well, that's because you don't have a printer."

Mom: "Oh. Well, what if I sent you back the documents and you print them out?"

Child: "Umm, that would be cool, but first, I still have the documents on my computer. Besides, if I print them out, how are you going to get them?

Mom: "Honey, think. If you print out the documents, you can send them back to my Yoohoo account from your computer machine. And how can you still have the documents if you sent them to me?"

Child: "Mom, I don't think that you fully grasp the...

Mom: "There's this thing that keeps popping up on my screen. Should I click on it? I wonder what will happen if I ...?"

Child: For God's sake, mother don't...Look, don't do anything. I'll be right over."

Anyway, now that you have gone away to college, you may have been close enough to come back home for the occasional weekend visit, and most of the major holidays where you could get a home-cooked meal, do some laundry and maybe score some cash.

The point is, your parents still talk about you even though you are not there. "High school was a real pain in the ass, but at least he/she showed up on our doorstep every now and again. You know, Martha, the next move our child makes will be the one where he/she doesn't come home any more."

That is a very sad thing for parents to endure. They have been losing you for the last ten years or so. Now that you're getting married, they have finally come to the realization that you are not a child anymore, but a grown adult embarking on a brand new chapter in your autobiography.

REAL ADVICE

And they know that after the wedding ceremony, you won't be back. For many parents, it is a sad time indeed. And here you are, all happy about it.

Speaking of letting go, I don't know how you were raised, but chances are, when you were tiny, daddy fixed your broken toys and maybe built you something while mom fixed your skinned knees and wiped your runny nose. As you grew older and you were able to do more things yourself, these occurrences became less and less frequent, but pop was still needed to make sure the fluids in your car were at the correct level, and the plugs were still throwing off plenty of spark. Mom still made sure you dressed warmly, and while you were attending college, a care package arrived at your door with some regularity.

They still had that mini van to tote you and your crew around, and they sat on those hard, cold high-school bleachers at every game you played in. For years, you probably thought that your parents attended your games because they loved you and hoped it would be you that hit the walk-off home run, or scored the winning goal in one of the championship games. Unfortunately, the real truth was that, yes they loved you, and yes, they were truly hoping that you would be the centerpiece of your team, but all the while, your parents were praying to their personal God: "Please Dear Lord, don't let my child be an asshole."

But now, now that you have a husband, he'll be the one changing the flat tire and making sure your plugs are throwing off the right amount of spark. Now that you'll have a wife, she'll be the one making sure you keep your doctor appointment and she'll be the one that makes sure that tie goes with that suit.

The parents are anxious, anxious about their child's happiness. Anxious about whether he or she is truly the right one for their precious child. Anxious about their child's quality of life that he or she will be living with the new partner. After all, up to this point, the parents have been involved in most of the big decisions regarding their child.

But choosing who to love and who to spend the rest of your life with is the most momentous decisions you have ever made without the help of your parents. This is because they couldn't be involved with who you ultimately give your heart to. That decision is made by you and you alone.

My Advice? Accept it all. It's all part of pageantry of getting married, isn't it? Both sets of parents are going through a lot of emotions right now, and they have an irresistible urge to jump in to give advice as well as money. You choose what to take and what not to take.

In case you haven't picked up on the nuances, take the money, not so much the advice. But there is (can be) an ineffective way and an effective way to handle all of this parental involvement.

My Advice? I've said it before, but it bears repeating: You and your future mate must present a united front. (That's Sun Tzu, again. You really need to read that book.) I know that you two talking about the wedding plans can be truly taxing on you both, so to combine those conversations with you two talking about how to handle each others parents can just add to the general overall craziness. But at some point, especially if things are getting out of hand, you both need to step in with the same expectations and desires.

REAL ADVICE

Remember those first meetings with the parents when you two were dating? Same advice here: Look 'em in the eye and say what you mean. And after you say it, continue to focus your gaze on them. That lets 'em know you are an adult, you know your own mind, and that is that.

Ahh, but who does the telling?

There's lots to say on this subject, and professional advice givers on such matters are not always in agreement as to how to handle standing up to the pressures the parentals bring to bear on you and your well laid plans.

My Advice? Sorry, it's too much of a mixed bag here (and very dangerous territory). My last piece of advice on having a united front is correct: have a united front. But who does the standing up to and who does the telling is something else entirely.

Here's an unlikely scenario to illustrate what I mean:

One set of parentals lets you know that everybody just loves polka music. They just happen to know of such a band who they heard play at the Elk's Club a few months back. The band would jump at the chance to play at your wedding reception. Best of all, the parentals are sure they could get them at a really good price.

Problem solved.

Now while saving money on the reception music is always a good thing, you both are into EDM and the Indie music scene. You have planned to hire a DJ, give him/her your hand chosen playlist, and have him/her go to town with it.

Controversy.

Now the parentals who suggested this polka music have spoken with the other set of parents and they simply love the idea. So now, four people are coming at you head on. Whatareyougonnado? Who speaks for the happy couple?

Well, if the bride speaks to her family separate from her betrothed, while the groom speaks to his family without his betrothed, this could be perceived as not much of a united front. It is a version of divide and conquer. You have split your forces, and are facing an enemy that is not only greater in number, but these are the very same people who control the world's economy.

Remember what I said much earlier in the show? It was something about the fact that you really don't know somebody until that first argument with them. Well, the same hold true with the fact that you really don't know somebody until you make an agreement with them. It can show here.

Maybe one set of parents gets one of you to thinking. "Hmm, polka music. Sounds better every time you guys say it." And since neither one of you are together propinquity-wise, the bride may say that her intended is making her play that EDM crap, and "There's nothing I can do about it." Same with the groom. He may cave under the pressure and take the easy way out, blaming it all on his intended, and "There's nothing I can do about it."

Oops.

Even if you go together to politely decline their offer, her parents will blame it on him, and his parents will blame it on her. This could be a battle neither one of you can hope to win. Both sets of parents will be at the least, disappointed, maybe even resentful. Both of you may feel badly about making the rents feel badly.

The point is, choose your battles wisely. Is the issue at hand something important enough to potentially cause a disruption in the group dynamic? Do you take Sun Tzu's advice? "If your enemy is superior, evade him. If angry, irritate him. If equally matched, fight, and if not, split and reevaluate."

My Advice? You (hopefully) have learned the art of compromising with your future mate. Take those lessons and apply them to any in-law pressure. If what they are proposing does not interfere with your plans or overall themes, listen. Parents have actually been known to come up with some good ideas. Better yet, if one of the mom in-laws comes up with some ideas about a pastry table with blueberry muffins and ladyfingers soaked in Kahlua, fine. Put her in charge. It will keep her busy, allow her to feel she is part of the process, and keep her out of your hair for a bit. "How's them pastries comin', ma?"

Look, there are no fast and hard rules to handle the future in-laws. This is something you both have to suffer through. Just remember that in the final analysis you are the ones getting married. After all the dust settles, you should both come out the other end much stronger for the experience.

Just keep in mind that old saying: "What doesn't kill you makes you stronger." Personally, I've always hated that statement, because unless you really are going to be dead in the next six months or so, and you really don't care what anybody thinks because you're going to be dead soon, what doesn't kill you almost always makes you just nuts.

My Advice? In so many aspects of our lives we can't go to the nearest referee and call for a 30-second timeout. "Janice, the boss wants to see you in his office."

"Oh shit."

But with dealing with unwanted, unsolicited, and many times bad advice, you actually can call for a timeout. Both of you commit to a day just by yourselves—no talking about the wedding. Just enjoy each other's company while you both attend a ball game, do the Sunday New York Times crossword puzzle, take a walk, or ride them Cialis horses on the beach. And no talking about anything connected to the wedding or the in-laws or for that matter, anything at all.

The Parentals After Marriage

Regardless of what you have been told, or have read, or have ruminating around in your head, life is not a thirty-minute sitcom. Mothers will not come to your house and put on a white glove and run their hands over the mantle. They will not look for dust bunnies under the couch or sniff the air and comment on the fact that you must have a cat somewhere. They won't start right off talking about you two starting a family.

But the truth is, they will very subtly look for any un-Liquid Golded coffee tables, artfully steer their vision to the underside of your couch for traces of those dust bunnies, and they will sniff the air. They may even gently steer the conversation into the realm of parenthood. They'll probably say something smarmy.

Not to be too much of a sexist here, but dad, while always being a human wrecking ball, can be a bit more predictable. However, he will somehow try and find out just how many power tools there are (A man ain't no man, he ain't got no power tools) and ask whether there's a ball game on the TV. Other than maybe checking on the fluid levels in your car, he's pretty good.

Regardless of your age and circumstances (financial and otherwise), the parents from both sides (even though you are now married and finally having sex that has been sanctified by the Holy Father) will still see you as a much younger and dependent person. They will still be more than willing to pass on all of their worldly knowledge. They will still mention that you could have done whatever you are doing at the moment a little differently. They will suggest. They will cajole. They will hover. This has been the way of the world for thousands of years and will be thus until the end of time.

Oh, and just wait until you do have that designer clone-baby.

Because of this non-evolution, after marriage, the parents from both sides tend to be judgmental about your home, your job, your clothes, your hair, etc.

Did you know that some team of researchers did some kind of study drawing a correlation between in-law satisfaction, and the longevity of a couple's marriage? Can you believe that? They actually took time off from doing really important scientific inquiry to descend into familial relations. Of course, I should be quite happy about this since if they didn't, I would have to leave this whole section out, and you would never learn how important it is to have good relations with the relations.

Anyway, what they found was pretty interesting. There were differences between the husband and wife in how they each reacted to and interpreted each other's relationship to their respective in-laws, but some cool data was (and here's that word again) extrapolated.

And here's the study: The researchers followed about 400 couples for a few years, and had both the husband and the wife rate the closeness of their relationship to the in-laws. I guess to keep it simple, the couples rated their satisfaction on a 1-4 scale.

Now the researchers, being, well, researchers, kept track of all of the data they were getting, including whether the couples stayed together. (This must have really been a long study.) Anyway, they found that when the wife's ratings were high (that meant she had a close relationship with her husband's parents), there was actually an increase in the probability of divorce (20% higher) than the wives who reported a not so close relationship with the in-laws.

Just the opposite was true with the husbands and in-law relationships. Of those husbands who reported a close relationship with his wife's parents, there was a 20% lower probability of divorce than those husbands that reported a not so close relationship.

Hmm.

Why, you ask? HellifIknow.

Actually, there are some interesting findings on this. When her husband really and truly puts in a good faith effort to bond with the Colonel and Martha, the young wife sees this as a sign of love for her. Remember what we talked about before, about how the husband and wife oftentimes have a different worldview concerning relationships. Because Jimmy is letting the Colonel whip his ass on the golf course, she sees all of this as his attempt to make her happy. Of course, the Colonel is happy too.

Now ain't we all content?

Ahh, but the wife's closeness with the in-laws doesn't always end up so happily. When she gets too friendly with her husbands parents, it can be interpreted as a sign of influence peddling and the inability to set appropriate boundaries. Men do not like, nor do they appreciate two women (his wife and his mother) sitting around talking about them. Especially while the two are sharing some of that tasty and tongue loosening Merlot.

So where do we go from here? Well, you have survived the parentals during courtship. You have both survived the wedding planning with the future in-laws flying all over the place like the monkeys in The Wizard of Oz. Now you must survive them in your marriage.

To do this effectively, we need to go back up two paragraphs. The wife's closeness to the in-laws doesn't work out well because the husband can see it as almost a betrayal. The husband is thinking that his wife is spilling the beans on private stuff, and that his mother is adding a generous dose of: "When Jimmy was growing up..." Trust me: men hate that.

How to circumvent this?

My Advice? Whether the study on in-law relations has any credibility or not, it is much safer to be ready for anything. First, it's important to set boundaries. This will be impossible to do rationally. If you think back, you and your mate have already had one or two dust ups concerning each other's parents. I can almost guarantee you that there will be more. As we talked about earlier, the nature/nurture things in all families is different and confusing and contain so many subtleties and contradictions, that it is hard, if not impossible, for someone outside the family to fully grasp and appreciate them.

So, you two will cross swords on this again, but you two must also discuss in-laws relations. Chances are, humans being humans, you two may never end up with the appropriate appreciation for each other's stands on these in-law matters, but at least you can never say, "Oh Jimmy, I really didn't know how you felt."

The point here is that both of you need to discuss relationships with the in-laws. You both need to act as traffic cops, keeping the flow of information moving without any rear enders. Hey, It's worth a shot. The only other options you two may have is either moving to the foothills of the Appalachians, or going completely off the grid. Attractive, but probably not doable.

Here is a possible scenario:

The wife returns from a nice visit with her mother in-law. She seems to be rather down.

"What's wrong, Babe? (He still calls his wife Babe because he's a newlywed. This too will change.)"

Well, your mom and I got to talking, and one thing led to another about how I'm handling this new marriage and all, and I said, "You know Mother Martha, it just seems to me that whenever we get together, you seem to find my inadequacies."

So your mom says, "Oh no my dear," I'm sure you are quite capable of finding your own inadequacies."

"Jimmy, I just hate this. I want to have a good relationship with your mother, but Goddamn, it's so hard. I need your help."

Big Jimmy now becomes Little Jimmy because he knows that talking to his mom about how she treats his wife is going to be a real bitch.

I remember when my daughter (daughter number one) became gravely ill and had to spend much time in the hospital. My wife and I pretty much lived there as well. My wife, being a registered nurse, took over the reigns as her overall health provider. Me? I assumed the role of guard dog.

So many relatives wanted to see her, and we were constantly inundated with requests from well wishers. Because of the nature of her illness, the strict schedule we all had to keep and her young age, visitors were always appreciated, but not always welcomed. I literally had to stand guard at the door to her room and on many occasions had to tell my in-laws that now might not be the best time to visit. And if it was a good time for a visit, there cannot be any crying or wringing of hands over her condition. In short, I was the "bad cop." I didn't relish this role, but it was one I had to play. By the way, daughter number one made a full recovery and is doing fine.

I tell you this story to illustrate a point: Sometimes Jimmy needs to be the wolf at the door. He has to stand up for his woman and be an advocate. Not that women are weak and constantly need to be propped up, but the truth is, when dealing with an in-law conflict, we all could use a bit of help in the deliberations.

Again with the nature/nurture. Jimmy knows his parents better than you, and even though he may be met with blank stares when he lets them know he doesn't appreciate they way they treat his wife, he will probably be defter in dealing with them. Besides, by hubby doing this on your behalf, it shows his parents that he has grown up and has assumed adult roles and responsibilities while showing you his respect.

Of course, all this could backfire (and it probably will) on you. If you have to harangue Jimmy to fix this problem, well, it's Saturday night, and what would Saturday night be without some kind of fight? Also, if Jimmy goes alone, it could put you in the role of "chicken" in the eyes of his parents. But then if you do go with him and let him do all the talking, after you leave, the in-laws will say to each other, "She put our Little Jimmy up to this, the bitch." Sometimes you really just can't win no matter how you play it. It's playground stuff.

However, this is not the time to pack it in and do nothing. Hurt feelings and personal slight, left unattended begin to fester, and things will only get worse.

My Advice? Have Big Jimmy do this by himself. It's not perfect, and it may not work as well as you would like it to, but as long as the husband doesn't revert back to Little Jimmy in front of his mom and dad, and wife doesn't have to nag him to death to go see them, this really is the best option in my eyes.

P.S. Should the husband actually do this, he needs to make sure the meeting with his parents is followed up by a personal visit or a phone call from the offending party to his wife. For her part, the wife needs to be gracious, but firm in her expectations as to how she is to be treated.

Good luck with that.

By the way (and not to dampen your spirits too much), some researcher at the University of Washington did another one of those studies (God, it's amazing they all have so much free time to do these things) on how men (husbands) react to the stress of conflict.

Pretty much the entire planet believes that men (generally speaking) are better at running headlong into one conflict (especially verbal conflict) or another, and is more comfortable with doing that than a woman might be. This may not be entirely true.

I don't really know how they did all of this, so don't ask me, but the research team hooked up married couples to an array of electrodes that gauged such things as heart rate, blood pressure and even adrenaline levels. Then they set the couples to fightin'. I don't know if they actually prodded them to fight, or they just sat outside of their windows and waited for the inevitable quarrel to erupt.

What they found was interesting. The study found that the male became physiologically (both in his mind and body) overwhelmed quicker that the wife. His pulse will beat faster, his heart rate will increase, and his body will begin pumping gallons of adrenaline throughout his system.

A couple of things may happen. He may remove himself from the verbal conflict to protect himself and others; he may completely shut down as a sort of defense mechanism;

or he may just pick up that frying pan and toss it in someone's direction. With men, you just never know.

But if Big Jimmy becomes Little Jimmy and goes totally slack jawed blank to protect himself, his wife (who put him up to all of this) is going to see him as a pussy. This is what is called, "The law of unintended consequences." Unintended consequences are oftentimes the result of something stupid we do when we time travel into the past that completely alters the future. Anyway, you two will probably have one hell of a fight later.

So, even though you're sitting there thinking, "Big Jimmy has got to handle this." He may not ultimately be the one. Personally, however, I'm not sure how valid the study really is. Not that I'm discounting the guys in the white lab coats. And that includes the guy who keeps checking to see whether the round block of cheddar cheese is ready yet. But at least it's something to consider.

But worse than any possible maltreatment by the in-laws, is one where somebody (or both of you) starts running off at the mouth about your marital relationship. Or your finances. Or the subject about having children. Or the uncertainty of your employment. Or pretty much anything that gives the in-laws an unfettered opportunity to judge their daughter- or son in-law.

Now, I am not saying you should lie about things, I'm just saying remain mute on these subjects. When and if one of you is asked about matters that are of a personal nature, remember the boundary thing. This is private stuff, and if you start bad mouthing your husband or wife, or complaining about this and that, God bless 'em, but the in-laws will swoop down on you two like avenging angels. And nobody needs that.

REAL ADVICE

My Advice? If you have to, bitch about your spouse to your dog or cat. It's so much safer.

Let's take a quick poll. Raise your hand if you have ever heard the following words come out of your intended's/spouse's mouth: " Don't take it so personally. That's just how my mom/dad is." "You're complaining about my mother? Have you met yours?" "I really don't see that as a problem, and if you see it as a problem, then something is very, very wrong with you." "Just ignore him/her." "Just whose side are you on anyway?" "I hate you."

Chances are, one of you guys have said these words to the other. You will fight about this. You will make up about this. You will fight again about this. It's the circle of life thing again. Just don't walk away from it.

The point to all of this "how to handle potentially deadly in-law situations," is to let you know that there are no easy or quick fixes, and oftentimes your collective ideas about "fixing" things just don't work. There are so many hues and intensities to these internecine war games we are often forced to play, that it has a tendency to become quite complicated, and what you are left with is called a pyrrhic victory. In case you are too tired to look it up, a pyrrhic victory is a win on the battlefield, but one with such a devastating cost, that it might as well have been a defeat.

My Advice? The only real advice I can leave you with is to repeat what has already been said: stand your ground, and present as much of a united front as possible. Be on the same page. Don't show fear or reluctance to confront your parents about how they treat your mate. Don't just show sympathy for your mate, empathize with him or her, because you should know by now how devastating words from the parentals can be. An old baseball saying may be prudent here: You win some, you lose some; some get rained out. But you dress for every game.

Here's one last piece of advice. Since you two may be constantly trying to find ways to counter real or perceived hostilities from your respective in-laws, might I suggest you both start taking fencing lessons? Don't laugh. Well, okay, go ahead and laugh. But not only will fencing allow both of you let off a little steam from time to time, but you'll learn really cool terms and phrases like: "attaque au fer," "contre-temps" and "esquive." These are defensive and offensive techniques that are used to deflect your opponents epees (swords) in close quarter combat situations. If you two can look at each other during trying times when the in-laws are giving one of you a hard time, and both say in unison, "Parade composee," they will never see the coupe de grace coming.

I'm just sayin'.

CHAPTER EIGHT

I Am Not Your Mother

or

Hey, You're Not Broken

Life is a mess. That's a fact. The stuff we need to do hardly ever turns out right.

You strip the entire bed down to the mattress and wash all of the bed sheets. We add a whole bunch of fabric softener, because there is nothing better than sleeping in a bed that smells springtime fresh. There's almost something "back to the womb" in all of this. After we are completely finished putting on all of those wonderfully clean smelling sheets and comforters, and have re-pillowcased all the pillows, then gently fluffed the last one and placed it ever so lovingly on our bed, we stand back and admire our handiwork. It's perfect. Life is perfect. We are perfect. That's when we see the mattress pad lying on the floor. Shit. We re-strip the damn bed and put it all back together again including the Goddamned mattress pad and then step back to look at our second attempt. Somehow, it never looks as good as it did the first time when we forgot the mattress pad. Shit.

REAL ADVICE

You wait in line at the bank. You desperately need some dough and you've got to be back at work in less than 20 minutes. Only two teller windows are open for the 50 people who also really, really need some money. Most of these people would have used the ATM, but there are at least 30 cars in line outside. And it's not even a holiday. Shit. Of course, waiting in a long line for money is not as bad as waiting in a long line at McDonalds for your Quarter Pounder and large fries. The truth is, if you are lucky enough to get your fries right out of the oil, McDonalds fries are delish. But once they get a little cool, they ain't so much. Money, on the other hand can be any temperature and still taste great (metaphorically, of course). The guy directly in front of us in line can never resist the urge to huff and puff and then turn around to tell us what the entire planet already knows, "You would think these people would put more tellers in the window." Then he lets out the little "Heh heh" laugh as if what he said was too funny. Like we can do anything about this long wait. You weakly feign a half smile in his direction. Don't talk to me. Shit.

The Big Guys from corporate are coming into the office after lunch. They will all meet in the conference room to go over those quarterly reports. It's your job to make seventeen copies of this 26 pager, bind them, label them and have them in the conference room by 2:00. Shit. It's not really a terrible problem for you because you are always asked to pretty much do the impossible. First you have to go over to the CFO's office and grab that report. She is not in at the moment, but if you leave your name and number, she will get back to you as soon as possible. You wait. And you wait some more. Finally she arrives and searches for the next twenty minutes or so when she finally remembers that she passed it along to the V.P. of Operations. Shit. You hunt him down. You get your file. You rush to the copy machine that is strategically placed on the other side of the building. You enter your secret copy machine number. This is when you discover that you have no copy paper. Shit. Because of the recent austerity measures your company has instituted, all copy paper must now be kept in the corner of your cubicle. And you only get 500 sheets at a time, with the maximum amount of 1,000 sheets per month. Shit. So you run back to your little cubicle and gather up all your remaining allotment of paper and literally run back to the copy machine (But first, you travel to Wanda's cubical and steal some of her paper because you don't have enough and Wanda's a bitch anyway.). You finally arrive at the copy machine only to see Wanda happily eating a donut and making copies. A whole boatload of copies. Shit. Worse, when you left to go to get some paper, you never cancelled your secret copy machine number. Shit. Wanda is now making hundreds of copies on your dime. Shit.

OK, so life is a mess. But that doesn't mean you two need to be. All it takes is a little effort on both your parts to lead a clean, healthy, dirt free life.

This is a chapter on household chores for newlyweds. Personally, I hate the word "chore." It conjures up such words as "drudgery," "onus" and "burden." Just look up that word in the dictionary and you will find other, similar crappy words such as: "headache," "grunt work," "toil," and "menial labor." Worse, you will also find the word, "responsibility."

There are other words less commonly used in place of the word "chore" that I like much better such as, "devoir" (Cuz it's French and sounds cool), "mission" (cuz it sounds like secret agent stuff), and "scutwork" (cuz, well, I like the way it sounds).

REAL ADVICE

Some other of my dislikes include the "job jar" and the "Honey-do" list. A job jar is like entering your name in a contest to see who will win the first prize of a new car, or the booby prize of cleaning out the kitty litter box. My apologies to Forrest Gump, but life is not like a box of chocolates. You always know you are going to draw the cleaning out of the kitty litter-box prize. And that damn Honey-do list. First, they are always written for the men, like they are totally incapable of any sense of cleanliness, style or grace. Honey-do lists are orders from headquarters and many men secretly find them offensive. What are we, ten?

Of course, some people do just fine with these things. If one of them is you, then God bless, and I wish you both many years of germ free cleanliness and dust free curio cabinets.

Chores Before Marriage

I wrote much earlier in this book about the millions of couples who live together before marriage. Because of this trend, millions of others like maybe you already have come to an understanding regarding cleanliness, maintenance, and repair work around the house and yard. This is a good thing. And if this is the case, you may be able to skip through this chapter rather quickly. However, I urge you to read it only because it will either confirm that the way you are dividing up household devoirs (God, how I love French) is the best solution, or become acquainted with other, more efficient and agreeable ways to do things. Plus, I sort of need to justify my existence here.

Anyway, while you two were dating, who would be responsible for what around the house or apartment probably didn't come up much if at all. Your future spouse maybe had a place, you may have had your own. You kept up with your stuff, your fiancé kept up his or her stuff. Simple.

But there are those things before your union that can give you a pretty good idea as to how things will be by looking at ... you guessed it: the parentals and your future partners tells. And this is where that nature/nurture part of life can show itself again.

Regardless of whether you two lived together before marriage and worked out ways to divide up the chores (there's that word again), the marriage situation makes things a little bit different. Maybe you two already have a place and are currently looking into a more permanent living situation. Or maybe you both have already purchased a new house or apartment. I don't know. But marriage is the real deal. This is serious stuff, and the quicker you two get a handle on who is responsible for what, the easier things are going to get.

Now to those signs of what is to come.

When you two were dating, each one of you found yourselves at the other's house at least a few times. First, take in the scene visually. Look around the house real casual like. What do you see? How does the house look to you? Regardless of any outdated furniture or appliances, does the house look pretty neat? If it's all a big mess, then that tells you that your future spouse was raised by wolves. Remember, he or she takes many of his or her cues from the parents. If they are a mess, then maybe your intended will be a mess too.

Also, look to see how each of the parents are dressed and how they split up the labor around the house. Is dad sitting around in some not too clean outfit complete with at least a two-day growth? Does mom look just a bit too harried? This could mean that daddy doesn't do much and leaves the socialisin', cookin', cleanin' and such to his wife. If possible, look into your future mates old (or current) bedroom. Mom may say, "We've kept it just like she left it." This may mean one of two things. It may mean that it was already clean and they didn't have to do anything with it; or it could mean that they are letting you know in the passive aggressive style of parents, that you two won't last very long and they are simply waiting for their little princess to come back home. You can tell a lot by just observing.

Again, another caveat here. On your first visit, everyone is (usually) on their best behavior. Mom looks pretty good. The house is in decent shape. Yard looks OK. Dad has showered and shaved. They are the picture of a modern-day middle-class family. It's the subsequent visits to the house that say a lot more. How's everything look? Pretty shitty? If this is the case, it is because they just don't give a shit about your presence anymore and they have gone back to their regular routines.

Next, just listen to how mom and dad interact and how they interact with their child. If you really listen, you can detect a whole lot of stuff, including information about how clean or messy your intended has been throughout his or her life, and whether that trend will continue.

Parents simply love to talk about their child, especially the growing up years. Does mom tell you stories about how she had to follow him or her child around the house, picking up after him or her? Is she still doing it? Does dad tell you, "Tried to teach him to how to change the plugs in the family car a while back. After we put out the fire, we had it towed to the junkyard. This is why to this day I have no eyebrows."

If you listen and observe on these visits, you will learn so much more than if you two just had a series of conversations about household responsibilities. Besides, one of you is going to lie about this category anyway.

Other tells as to how it's going to be cleanliness wise after marriage include watching your future mates table eating habits, visiting the dorm room or his or her apartment, how he or she dresses, and most importantly, his or her car.

As Americans, we really love our cars. At least, we seem to spend a whole lot of time in them. The folks at Arbitron say that on average, we spend about two and one-half hours in them each day. Those of us who are above the age of 18 spend over 18 and one-half hours in our cars each week. That potentially could add up to 50,000 hours driving around in a circle that has become our life. That equals out to about nine years of our life we spend in our cars, driving the equivalent of three trips to the moon. Of course, they go on to say that three of those years during our lifetime of driving will be spent at stoplights.

For those of you who need a little perspective on this, comparatively, we will spend about ten minutes per day pooping. That equals out to about three years of pooping in our lifetime. If you noticed, that's about the same amount of time we spend at stoplights in our cars. If we could only set our pooping schedules to coincide with all those traffic lights, we could save a whole shitload... sorry, sorry, sorry.

Same thing can be said about how much time we spend naked. Come to find out that we spend about two and one-half years naked. So... if we could just be naked when we're pooping at the stoplight, think how many total years we could spend on other stuff.

REAL ADVICE

But you are newlyweds (or about to be), and you don't want to hear all of that. So hear these depressing statistics. You will probably only spend a total of about 14 days in kissing for your entire life, and there are so many variables about having sex, who knows how long you will spend on having it. But if you need to know, the average sex part generally lasts only about 13 minutes. You do the math. But do not include the sex time you have had, you know... with yourself. It's only fair.

Back to the car thing. Now the information I am about to give you is only anecdotal. No research team from the I'm Smarter Than U. did a study on this, but generally speaking, the guy is the one who usually drives a real shit box. It hasn't been washed since the last owner did it. The only instrument that works is the radio (and it's usually only the door speakers that are all fuzzy sounding). It's totally trashed with fast food wrappers and ketchup stains. There is a coating of dirt and dust from the top of the dashboard all the way to the back window. It stinks. Occasionally, a cockroach can be seen skittering from one empty McDonald's wrapper to another. The engine runs pretty decent, but there are squeak and squeal noises coming from the undercarriage. This is why we call it a shit box.

A young woman's car just might be in the same shape as his, but without all of the dirt and dust covering the interior, and it usually smells pretty good. I don't know why that is, but again, this is just anecdotal.

Since we spend all those hours each day in our beloved automobiles, if your future mate treats it poorly, that is also another one of those tells. He or she is a slob and that slobiness will follow him or her into your new house.

Now I know that when you two met and fell in love, then made plans to marry, you probably didn't have any preliminary conversations about who is going to do what around the house. And let's be frank about it. Who is going to do the dishes or dust the tables ranks with: "Will you still love me when I start wearing Depends?" conversations. There were so many other things to discuss and dream about, and the crappy parts of the day-to-day mechanics of living together was not something either one of you are or were focused on. It's not that both of you pushed back the conversation about this subject; it's just that this was one of those things that would take care of itself.

Just remember what I said much earlier. Newlywed couples will fight more about household chores than they will about financial matters. Why, you ask? This is because household chores are everyday items on the agenda, that need to be addressed every day, and money problems can be put off until the next paycheck. Money fights will be worse, but chore fights will be more frequent.

My Advice? Get the conversation going whenever you feel it's an appropriate time, but before you two walk down the aisle together. Like so many other issues, who's taking care of what isn't very sexy (unless part of that two and one-half years you will spend naked in your lifetime is spent cleaning the house in the nude). But getting this part of your life together straightened out is essential.

Please, just know this, it has been said that all plans are perfect until you put them into action. It's the same thing with chores. Both of you will make promises and commitments that will fall by the wayside, so don't be too harsh on your partner. Work was a real bitch today. You are really tired. You just cleaned out the kitty litter box before you went to work today. It's hot. You're hungry.

There's a movie you want to watch. Don't talk to me. Where's the wine? Where's the beer? There's no laundry soap. Forget the dishes, we can use the paper plates. I hate you.

Chores After Marriage

Before we get into the specifics of the division of labor after marriage part, there's a couple of housekeeping things you need to do after getting back from the honeymoon (assuming you had enough cash stuffed in those wedding reception envelopes).

My Advice? As soon as you return to your home from whatever post-wedding trip you could afford, unpack and put everything away all nice, nice. Do the laundry and hang everything up. I fully realize you are exhaustipated and all each of you want to do is flop down on the couch and sleep while the TV drones on and on, but don't. Because if you don't, you are going to have all your crap lying around the house making a total mess. You may have nothing to wear to work on Monday. And this is how you know that partially, all the best fun you ever had or will have is over: you have to go back to work in a couple of days. Shit.

My Advice? Depending on the size of your wedding and the size of family and friends' wallets, you also have a bunch of gifts and mementoes from the wedding that were transported over to your place by the in-laws while you were away (See, in-laws can actually be quite useful). Put this stuff away too. If you have special keepsakes that mean a lot to you, put them in one of your cabinets for display, or just store them in a safe waterproof place. Put all those wedding gifts where they belong, including that Wal-Mart blender that will soon blow up in your face.

My Advice? Make a decision. If it's something that doesn't trip your and your new spouse's trigger, toss it. It can be brutal, but it's necessary. Put the pictures from the honeymoon and the wedding in their respective albums so you can show them to everyone who comes over to visit you. And I include the FedEx guy. If you don't, you're gonna lose them. Do it.

My Advice? One other thing your in-laws can help with is the overflow. Give them all the stuff you don't have room for, or stuff you are not sure about. Trust me, they will love the gesture and will be more than happy to give your stuff a good home.

My Advice? I shouldn't have to tell you this, but you would be surprised at how many newlyweds make this really stupid mistake. If you still have something from your past that includes poems, photos, mementoes, or mix tapes from a former lover or six, throw them away now. Why in the hell do you still have them anyway? The worst thing that can happen is that your spouse will accidently find these little reminders of your past life and start peppering you with impossible to answer questions. GoodLordAlmighty, ditch them. I mean really ditch them. I burned all of mine. Literally. I set fire to them. Admittedly, it didn't make a big fire, but big enough so that you could roast a few marshmallows from it.

My Advice? I sincerely hope you got a lot of cool gifts from all the folks in attendance at the wedding and reception. I am also hoping that those who couldn't make it at least picked something from your bridal registry and sent it to you. Among those great wedding gifts are going to be shitty gifts and gifts that are duplicates.

REAL ADVICE

You have some options here. Take them all back to the store (if possible) and get some cash. Give them back to their rightful givers in the hopes that they will then ask you what you truly need and get it for you. You can donate all the overflow, duplicates and shitty presents to a recognized charitable institution. And as the cavernous-mouthed Suzi Orman would say, "It's tax deductible."

My Advice? If you can help it, don't put these duplicates or unwanted wedding gifts on eBay or have a garage sale to rid yourselves of them. Aunt Tillie will see her gift and feel really bad about all of this. Or worse, your mom will find out that you are selling Aunt Tillie's palm tree placemats and let you know in her passive aggressive way how much you have broken every one's collective hearts.

The great thing about getting all your stuff in order as soon as you get back, besides not having a mess for the next six months, is that even if you two have not decided on how the household chores are to be done, both you and your spouse can run around together to accomplish all of this. You are both free to pick and choose what you want to do and when you want to do it. This is one of those rare times where both of you are on the same page and don't mind sharing your fair share of the duties. You really are doing this for each other's happiness.

Author's Note: A caveat here if I may: Not to be sexist or anything, but don't leave the wedding photo album to the husband. The reasons should be obvious.

Again, just sayin'.

Once you are married (hopefully to each other), it's now time to divide up all those chores you both may have been doing solo. There are two of you, so there's bound to be twice the mess. If you got a cute little puppy, more mess.

I know I'm repeating myself here, but unless you guys are really the only perfect couple in existence, you will both find pretty quickly just how fast all those little understandings about housework can fall apart. "Look, you said you would..." "You promised..." "I can't do this; could you just..." "Get off your lazy fat ass and..." "I hate you."

My Advice? Ease up. If you invest in the "We need to clean this dump up" too heavily, and your life partner is not quite cooperating, someone is going to put the horse head from The Godfather on the other's side of the bed. Someone is going to be bobbing and weaving to avoid the frying pan aimed at their head. Someone will be eating stale dry toast all served up on a piece of tree bark and drinking water from the dog bowl.

I say ease up because no matter how many promises are made beforehand and no matter how much prompting is needed, not everybody views housework on the same level. Add to that, the possible frustration caused between you two because things are not happening soon enough or correct enough. All this has a tendency to cause much unneeded friction.

The truth is, at a certain point, not only will everything get done, but without even fully realizing it, the two of you will probably divide all of this household labor stuff along traditional lines (Congratulations. You are now your parents.). I know we are a good ways into the 21st century, but it's a fact. In all likelihood, the man will be in charge of automobile repairs, taking out the trash, killing off all the unwanted bugs, cooties and spiders, lawn mowing, and anything that requires the use of some power tools.

REAL ADVICE

In all probability, the wife will usually be in charge of the cooking and the kitchen. The man will cook only if it's a barbecue and open flames are required. She will be the planter of flowers and shrubs. The woman will also be in charge of the laundry and the bathroom(s). What is it about guys and really gross bathrooms? She will also be the one who shops for food and while she may split the vacuuming duties with her mate, she will do the dusting and curtain straightening.

This can all be interpreted as sexist stereotyping, I get it. But one of the problems about stereotyping is that many times they're true. It's like a lot of our myths and stories that we were told when we were children. Often, they come from something that really did happen, but through the years and centuries of being told, they have been embellished to one degree or another, but there's always a grain of truth to them. Same with falling into traditional roles: "I'll kill it and bring it home. You skin it and cook it."

Nobody's fault.

This of course doesn't mean that Big Jimmy can't do laundry. Or plant some rose bushes. Or iron. Or dust. It doesn't mean that our Little Janice (or as mommy-in-law likes to call her, "Janet") is incapable of barbecuing. Or changing the oil in the car. Or swatting flies and catchin' varmints. Or baiting a hook.

It's just that it is almost inevitable that we fall into what has been familiar to us for most of our lives. And if you are at least sort of like the rest of humanity, what you witnessed from your parents as you grew up still has the capacity of shaping you today. Nurture is a hard thing to transcend. Dad did this and this. Mom did that and that. And as much as we pretend that we are not our parents...we are.

Sorry. As human beings, we tend to choose many of our roles along the gender lines we saw our parents follow. We also tend to put ourselves in charge of those household duties that we are good at, or the jobs we did for our parents when we still lived at home.

Remember two things I have said before: One is that when you both were just dating each other, you did almost everything together (the hormone stuff). You both probably cooked for one another, you may have help clean each other's place, and you both probably went shopping together. Even after you got married, you both pitched in as a team to get all the wedding gifts together and your new digs in order. You gelled.

And here's the second thing: You're married now. And I don't care how long you two may have lived together before the wedding, marriage, in and of itself changes things.

Welcome to the big leagues.

One thing about this shopping together: It's quite probable that early on in your married life, you two will shop together. It's got something to do with not being able to separate yourselves from one another, because you are so damn much in love. But sooner or later this will change. One of you will pretty much take charge of the grocery shopping and for the next several decades, that is how it will be. You two won't regularly shop together again until you are both really, really old.

Nothing wrong with it, it's just me being prescient.

So as you two settle in, roles begin to be defined more clearly. There will always be exceptions, but she will cook and he will take out the garbage. She will clean and he will look for any bear activity in the backyard. She will do the laundry, while he puts your cars head gasket in the bathtub. In it's own special and natural way, it's really quite a beautiful thing, is it not?

My Advice? Be bendy. Just because you two came to an understanding or agreement or drew straws or had some legal documents drawn up, doesn't mean it's gonna happen. It's like Captain Quint said in Jaws: "...sometimes the shark would go away. Sometimes he wouldn't go away." It's the same thing with work around the house. Sometimes you make it go away. Sometimes you don't make it go away.

Being bendy means that sometimes one of you needs to step in and do the chore your spouse normally does without any acrimony. Even if it is meant to just get your mate going. You may suck at it, but what the hell.

Here's some free advice for both of you: Don't be that, "Hey, you missed a spot. Hyuck, Hyuck." person.

There is absolutely nothing worse when you're sweating and toiling on some stupid labor-intensive household project, then having your spouse interrupt you with: "Why are you doing it that way?" "Why don't you..." "Did you remember to..." "Ya know, you should..." stuff.

ChristAlmighty—chores. Nobody but nobody gets married because their future partner is good at housekeeping or cooking or car repairs or anything that entails manual labor around the house. It just isn't done. Maybe it was true back in the 1800s, but not anymore.

Chores will lead to fights, yes, but sitting around divvying up the labor pool with, "I'll do this and you'll do that." just doesn't always work as promised in the real world. Neither do job jars or "Honey-do" lists. Accept it and move on. Besides, isn't this why we have children? In a few years, they will be the ones cooking and cleaning and taking out the garbage. Thank God for the little children.

Which leads us to our last bit of advice. The kids.

CHAPTER NINE

You Want To Have How Many?

This chapter, though logistically difficult, will be constructed pretty much the same way as the previous four. But because of so many variables and conditions that exist with living arrangements these days, it's difficult to talk (write) about the children before marriage. Time was, discussing children before marriage was not necessary (except for that whole "birds and bees thing." And who didn't just love going through that experience?). These days we speak a lot about blended families, adopting Vietnamese babies and such because of how times have changed. But the fact is, nowadays, many of you out there in "Reading This Book Land," may already have children either from one of the many premarital sexual unions with your soon-to-be or just now married-to spouse; or you may have a child or two (or more) from a previous marriage.

If so, that's fine. It is very common these days that couples who are soon to be married to come already assembled. It's kind of like getting those free batteries included with the present you just purchased.

Why is it, by the way, that most manufacturers include those off-name batteries in the box that last for, like five minutes? I mean, if you are spending 30 or 40 bucks on a gift, they should at least throw in a few Copper Tops.

Anyway, children.

Before we start pulling out our wallets to show each other a picture of our kids, let me give you a few interesting stats on childbearing and associated parenting information that I have come across in my travels. The sources of the following information come from a wide variety of experts (much of it from the Center for Disease Control, believe it or not) and other authorities on the whole birthing babies thing. I personally cannot attest to how true everything is, but it does give you pause to at least think about some of the ramifications.

1. By age twenty-five, 44 percent of women have had a baby, but just 38 percent have actually gotten married.

2. 48 percent of all first births are now to women who remained unmarried.

3. Most unwed mothers are not teen mothers (there goes that stereotype).

4. Only 23 percent of all unmarried births are to teenagers.

5. 39 percent of couples who live together and have a child break up within 5 years.

6. A 2011 government report estimated that the average US family spends $295,000 to raise a child from birth to age 17. Of course, then there's college where the parents will spend another $295,000 in just four short years. So the rents are now about a

half a million in debt with a child who has just acquired a Bachelor's Degree in Puppetry.

7. Most babies are born in the month of September on a Tuesday.

8. Only 23% of women will gain 20 or less pounds during their pregnancy. The rest of you (77%) will add anywhere from 21 to 40 (or more) pounds. About a third will increase their weight somewhere between 21 and 30 pounds. Yikes.

9. The ratio between male and female babies is about one to one, with the male babies just slightly more "popular." Been that way for about 60 years.

10. Some study by some researchers living somewhere submitted something to *Population and Development Review* (it's some kind of professional journal) about parents over the age of 40. These parents report that they are much happier than parents under 30. The article went on to state that for people under 30, happiness declines with each additional child. But for parents between the ages of 40 and 50, the number of children has no impact.

Huh?

This is why no one outside of academia has heard of *Population and Development Review*.

The Children Before Marriage

See, here's where it gets tricky because there are so many possible scenarios. However after surveying all of the many

REAL ADVICE

permutations, there are 4 more "common" possibilities about children and marriage:

1. You two fooled around and fooled around and fooled around some more. Somebody got pregnant.

   Oops.

   So, you two talked about it and fought about it and then fooled around again. After all, ya can't get pregnant again, can ya? You both decided that you would get married because, well, isn't that what you are supposed to do?

2. One of you is pregnant. But because of so many other Goddamn obligations in both of your lives (including the student loans), you two decided that you would just live together for now, and get married later either before somebody started to show, or just after the baby is born. Either way, you got about six months to decide. Yikes.

3. One of you (or maybe both of you) has already been married before and from that previous marriage, a child (or children) has been produced. You are obviously both aware of this because there always seems to be a rather short person constantly hanging out with you wanting something to eat.

4. You have both been dating each other, you fell in love, and decided to get married. Neither one of you has children. You are both starting your marriage with each other unencumbered (except for that damn student loan stuff).

Look, these four scenarios do not represent all that could be going on in your lives regarding children before you get married. There could be many more plots and subplots at play: One of your relatives might have come across some hard times and left their little one with you to raise; one of you may not be able to conceive; one of you may have a genetic disease that is likely to be passed on, and you are reluctant to have a child because of it; considering your respective lifestyles, both of you are absolutely 100% sure that children will never be a part of your future together. And so on and so on. But I only chose the above four possibilities because they represent the most common stories.

Let's start with the easiest and still most common scenario: you are young, just getting started in this marriage business, and neither one of you have any children that you know of or will admit to.

OK, let's see. Got my toothbrush, some peanut butter, bug repellant, clean underwear, and some Tic-Tacs. Have I got everything? It's strange, somehow I keep getting this feeling that I forgot something. Hmm. What the hell could it be?

Oh yeah, wait, did we have that talk about having children yet?

So it begins.

I'm using this little traveling analogy to gently let you know that before (long before) you start your car and head down the road to marital bliss, I really, really hope you had that talk with your spouse about where babies come from. Plus, just because I truly care about you, I hope you filled the gas tank and had the Colonel check your fluids.

REAL ADVICE

If neither one of you has had that talk about having children by the time the proposal came around, you are both headed for one of those "Falling Rocks" and "Cliff Ahead " signs I spoke of much earlier in this book. In short, you are going to get the shit knocked out of you very soon.

Why do I say this? Well, it's my book and I can say anything I want. But more to the point: in spite of everything, chances are, you would probably marry someone with an Irish temper (Chapter Five). You would probably marry someone who ain't got no money and can't handle finances (Chapter Six). You would probably marry someone who your family will always disapprove of (Chapter Seven). You would probably marry someone who could care less about a clean house (Chapter Eight). But would you marry someone who wanted three, maybe four children when you don't want any? Or vice-versa? Or anything in between?

Hence my, "...you are going to get the shit knocked out of you very soon." statement.

There are so many things you two can compromise about: fights and disagreements, financials, in-law relations and household duties. But this, should we have children, and if so, how many and when thing can really make that argument about how the toilet paper should be hung situation pale by comparison. If you two can't agree on the baby issue, trust me, it can be a real marriage killer.

As humans, we often fool ourselves. "If I mix ammonia and bleach to clean the bathroom floor with all the windows and doors shut, everything should be just fine and super clean and fresh smelling." "If I use a little gasoline to start the barbecue, it will speed up the whole process and make the food taste that much better." " If I mix 151 with some milk, my stomach should be OK." None of the aforementioned bright ideas ever work. Believe me on this: I've tried the gasoline thing.

But if you two cannot agree on raising children, do not automatically think that with time will come change. He/she says no to children, but that doesn't mean forever, does it? The fact is, maybe that's true, and maybe it isn't. Like Winnie the Pooh said, "You can never tell with bees."

My Advice? The only salient advice I can give you on this one is to talk it all out. I mean really, really talk it all out. On this one, neither one of you can afford to swing and miss, or be wrong and misunderstood. And if you both agree on whether to have children, and how many and when, make sure you are both solid with your decisions. Allow me to quote another famous American: Davy Crockett, who said, "First make sure you are right, then go ahead." You know, Davy was a man ahead of his time. He just doesn't get as much love as he should. Probably the whole raccoon hat thing.

Of course, the big question is, "How do I/we make sure I/we are right?" In truth, neither of you can. Remember what I have already said about never really knowing someone until you make an agreement with them. Life happens, and that's a fact. Things change, get in the way, mutate, and often just don't turn out the way anyone expected they would. It's never more true than with long-term planning.

Time was, children just kind of showed up in many marriages. Many married couples back then just "had them" in the natural course of time. Nowadays, for many reasons, married couples are more adept at planning their families, as well as starting a bit later than their parents did.

REAL ADVICE

This pre-planning has proven to be more successful than just churning out babies without much forethought.

Author's Note: Now again, while I'm not trying to absolve myself of any advice-giving responsibilities, I would be way out of my depth if I started giving out free advice on whether or when or how many babies you two should have. In the other four parts of this book, I didn't mind so much in giving out advice regarding money, in-law relations, fighting, and chores. They are so much more concrete. But birthin' babies? While you can plan and plan and plan some more, having little ones and all the things that go with them, is a particularly personal choice.

However, all is not lost. While I can't give you specific advice on starting a family, I can give you some talking points for your consideration. In your pre-marriage discussions about children, I strongly urge you to take these points and check them off. I have even listed them below so you won't have to try and find that pencil in your junk drawer. Just remember: honesty, brutal honesty is extremely important here.

1. Why do you/we want to have children?

2. How do we make accommodations to our current/future unencumbered lifestyle?

3. Can our chosen careers accommodate a child at some point?

4. How can we get to a place where we are secure enough financially?

5. How will having a child reflect on our marital relationship?

6. Do we/can we agree on our parenting styles?

7. How many?

The list is by no means complete. But I figure if you to can get all the way to number seven before you get married, you've accomplished more than just about anyone else.

My Advice? Talk about it. I know, I know, all of us advice givers keep telling you to talk everything pretty much to death. But this time we *really* mean it. As much as so many things will change over the course of your marriage, you can't be ready and prepared for every contingency. But both of you being able to agree at least in principle on the above seven baby points will greatly increase your probability of success.

Just keep in mind that while most of the other issues on your to-do list are finite and concrete, having children and raising a family is so much more emotional than anything else you two will encounter. Make sure that the tangible stuff (finances, support systems, et al) are rock solid, then make sure that both of you are emotionally rock solid before you take that next leap.

In short, grow the f**k up. Sorry. It had to be said.

Of course, not every couple is in the same situation. It's quite possible that one or both of you will be getting hitched to someone that comes to you with a child from a previous liaison or previous marriage. This is what we all call a blended family.

In case you have not been reading too much of late (with, of course, the exception of this book), or you haven't been watching your fair share of those PBS nature films, let me just say that the animal kingdom (which we humans are part of) is replete with blended families that don't turn out so well.

The lion will, (pretty much always) kill those cute little cubs that are not of his own making (sometimes even if they are). This is called infanticide in zoological terms. Filial infanticide is when they kill their own offspring. Even the horse, that majestic and truly beautiful animal that eats hay and oats and grasses, will do the same. If a new stallion takes over a herd of mares, he will stomp all those cute little baby horses to death, thus wiping out all vestiges of the last leader. Jeez Louise. Who would have thought that a horse would do this?

Truth is, even those happy-go-lucky dolphins have been known to do this, and the primates (chimpanzees, apes, etc.) also are guilty.

Now obviously, I am not saying that anyone should let "nature take its course." If you marry (or are about to marry) into a blended family situation, do not—I repeat— do not do what the lions and horses do. Be more like the squirrels and elephants that take in strays and orphans as a matter of course. Are we all clear on this? Don't be lions and horses. Be squirrels and elephants. I really don't want to get sued here because I gave some misunderstood advice.

But let's face it. Blended families can be a tremendous burden for either the bride or groom. You are not the "real" father. You are not the "real" mother. The child doesn't look like you. The child is a boy and you really wanted a girl. The child isn't as handsome or pretty as you would like. The child is not an infant and can already walk and talk and you totally missed the joy of watching it all happen. Since the child can already walk and talk, your life just got 10 times busier. The child is about two years old and you read somewhere that a human's basic personality is pretty much formed by that age so whatever you do to try and mold the child will be useless. Shit.

The child already has a father or a mother who will now be in the picture. Forever (not to mention the "other" set of grandparents). Visitation rights need to be addressed. You are expected to love a child that you have no genetic connection with and treat it like it was your own. Does your partner show deferential treatment to his/her child, forsaking you? In other words is some jealousy involved? What happens the very first time you reprimand the child (who is not yours) in front of your spouse? Will he or she support you in this, or will it all just all fall apart?

Whew.

My Advice? Patience. And go slow. Nobody spent their growing up years thinking, "I hope when it's time for me to marry someone he/she will already have a couple of kids that I can just love to death." Some people are cool with this at the outset. Some are not. Thrusting a child on your mate or potential mate can be quite tricky.

While I am quite aware that it is fashionable to accept and embrace virtually everything we humans come in contact with, I am also quite aware that we are humans and not as far advanced as we think we are. We still make fun of fat people. We still tell racist and sexist jokes (and laugh at them too). We still believe that blonds and Polaks (that's how it is spelled in Polish) are quite stupid. We still show our homophobic tendencies. We try and try and try some more to become better at being human on a daily basis, and most of us truly mean well, but we fall short about every ten minutes or so. We just do.

REAL ADVICE

Accepting a third party into your relationship that you had nothing to do with and can't control could be one of those times where you fall short. If you are the one with the child, don't naturally assume that your partner will welcome him/her with open arms. Even though your partner may love you very much, it doesn't always follow that your partner will automatically love the child "this very minute."

If you are a woman reading this, don't introduce your child to every guy you date. "Honey, this is my friend, John." It will only confuse your child seeing so many boy friends in your life and may leave the impression on him or her in later years that you are a hooker. "Boy," the now grown up child tells his therapist, "Mom sure had a lot of friends named John."

Introducing your child to all of the men you may be dating, and having those relationships end, may introduce or reinforce feelings of abandonment by the child, leading to a whole host of other problems.

None of these scenarios are good.

If you are a man reading this, don't assume that just because she is a female type woman that her womanly nurturing side will automatically kick in and she will immediately scoop up your little rascal in her arms and begin breast-feeding your five-year-old. She is just as likely to take one look at your offspring and think, "Man, he makes ugly babies."

Not so good either.

Now...some more advice should your mate already have a child. This advice is male and female friendly so it applies to whomever is reading this book.

If the love of your life hasn't beaten a hasty retreat after learning that you have a child, take the following steps to at least help in the transition of blending. By the way, whenever I am using our Wal-Mart blender, and the recipe says I need to puree whatever it is I'm making, I never just hit the puree button first. I always hit the slowest speed first, then keep pushing the buttons until I hit the fastest. Don't know why, I just do. I do the same thing with the eggbeater.

Anyway, make sure the meeting between your love and your child is not done right away. Give your relationship some time. Make sure you two have a future before any interaction takes place. And to be on the safe side, introduce your love to your child as your friend...special friend, new friend, old friend, whatever. Just make sure you don't say that "your friend" is the reason you no longer come home at night to tuck you in. This introducing as a friend business takes the pressure off everyone just in case things don't work out and nobody tries too hard to make a stupid first impression.

My Advice? Again, go slowly, and be steady. Don't try to manufacture some way to ingratiate or insinuate yourself artificially into the child's life. Remember, the child in question has been living without you for quite some time now and has done remarkably well. You cannot win the affection of a child. You have to earn it. Also, the child could be without a mother or father because of a divorce. You show up, then disappear, or make promises you can't deliver; well... you might as well bring out the analyst's couch right now.

Do your best (not always possible, but damn, at least try) to involve yourself in what the child likes to do. If it's board games, fine, play some Monopoly. Video games? Fine, play some. As time goes by, outdoor trips to an amusement park, the animal sanctuary (the zoo), a ball game will help you get to know the child on a deeper level. Just as an aside, try not to go to the movies together. Even though both of you may enjoy 97 minutes of watching cartoon penguins getting into all kinds of mischief, unless you are a teenager making out with your girlfriend on a Saturday night, watching a movie together is not the best way to get to know someone. It would be better to introduce the child to Texas Hold-em.

One caveat here, if I may. Never, and I mean never try to buy your way into the child's heart. Just like lighting the barbecue with gasoline, this will surely backfire on you. In the same way you won your lover's heart, you have to sustain the relationship with the child the same way you got it: with honesty. Buying children's affections will not last for long and will cause much bad juju in the home.

The Children After Marriage

There is a reason I put children as the last thing on the advice list. It is because if you got through your marriage and honeymoon with only a few dents and scratches, had your first fight, went through all the crap with the in-laws, found a way to at least have some decent credit and have given some thought to retirement, and finally figured out which one of you is going to mow the lawn on a semi-weekly basis, well, then you might just be ready to have a child...or two...or maybe more.

One more set of interesting set of statistics here if I may:

Back in the 1970's, the average age for first-time wedded mothers was 21 years old. Nowadays, that number is over 25 years of age.

Why do I bring this up? I do it to help take any pressure off of you and your spouse to conceive during the wedding reception.

Hopefully, you two have come to a firm agreement on having children. Hopefully too, both of you have agreed at least in a general sense about when and how many and under what conditions.

I came across an article some time ago concerning one half of a newly married couple waxing philosophical about the possibilities of having/not having children. It was about a woman (I forget her name) being interviewed (I forget the name of the magazine) about wanting to live life uninterrupted. She even used the phrase: "to live life uninterrupted." In the interview she said she was focused on traveling as much as possible, renting a sports car just for fun, trying out new restaurants, seeing all the first-run movies she wants and — hey, why not — having sex in every room of their house. She mentioned everything from sleeping late on Sunday mornings to taking off on a European jaunt.

The article didn't say whether she planned on including her husband in all of these activities, especially the having sex in every room of the house idea.

Yes, it sounds like a pretty good lifestyle this woman envisions—and it is. But let's be honest, while some of these things are doable, most of them are not for most of us. Again, brutal honesty is needed here. Raise your hand if you can drop everything and take off on a European jaunt next week. Raise your hand if you are going to rent a really cool sports car and drive to Daytona Beach to catch one of those multi-colored, multi-dimensional sunsets while the gentle ocean breeze falls soothingly on your now golden brown skin as you dreamily sip your Cuba Libre. Raise your hand if you plan on having sex in every room in your house... well that one, yeah.

The point is that many childless couples like to think that no good will come from having children regarding their freedoms. But even without a little one to bounce on your knee, you are no longer free. In fact, you may have not been free for some time. You have a job. For one reason or another, you are required to show up there at least five days a week. And, they want you to work all eight hours. You have a spouse. He or she requires you show up all seven days. You owe money to a lot of entities. They require a payment every month for the next 60 years or so. You have this obligation, and that obligation. You have friends and families that require a great deal of attention especially when you don't want to give it. You have a pet or two that require feeding and to be taken for walks every now and then. You are dealing with a lot of stuff.

Ahh, it's cool to be an adult, isn't it? You've waited all your life to be one, only to find this.

Shit.

Oh yeah, before I forget: This is strictly aimed at the men who might be reading this book. If you happen to be a woman, you may skip ahead a bit. I need to privately speak to the boys for a minute.

Boys, let's talk breasts.

Yes, those two wonderful things your wife has that you don't (until you are about 50 years old and they start budding one fine morning). Breasts. Those two wonderful things that, when you hit your teen years, you swore to all of your friends that if you had breasts, you would never leave the house again. You would just lock yourself in your room and have at it.

Anyway, nature has a way of evening things out in the universe. The same forces that bring you the hurricane and a tsunami or two, also brings new and improved versions of your wife's breasts. Mother Nature can be sweet, can't she?

Now when your sweet beloved is pregnant, everything gets bigger—her stomach, her legs, her feet, her thighs— everything. In the latter stages of her pregnancy, you may find it easier to just look away when she tries to bend over. Because everything about her is so damned huge, you don't necessarily notice her enlarged breasts. And let's be honest, guys, this is probably the first time since you were what, 11 that you didn't get turned on at the sight of breast flesh.

Ahh, but after the little one is born and all that nasty stuff that comes along with it is cleaned up by the nurse or the midwife, you notice something a bit different. Things have swollen up top.

Yay.

But hold on. Everything else has changed too. I'm speaking of the child she just gave birth to. Childbirth changes a lot of things which we will discuss a bit later in this chapter, and that includes access to her fun parts (actually, your fun parts. Your field of dreams so to speak). And although you have always been pretty proud of your wife's looks (breasts), you are totally impressed with what Mother Nature has sculpted (breasts).

REAL ADVICE

I can see you now, dropping to your knees, praying to your personal God that your wife's cup size will always remain thus.

Pig.

The fact is boys (and take it from someone who knows a great deal about this new breast sensation), you may not have the all-access pass to them that you used to. See, the milk has come in. Her breasts are swollen initially with what is called colostrum. A woman's breasts produce something called colostrum beginning during pregnancy and continuing throughout the early days to help keep the baby healthy. Colostrum is quite easy to digest, and therefore is said to be the perfect food for your new child. It is also low in volume (Think teaspoons rather than ounces), but it is high in concentrated nutrition for the newborn. Good news for those boys who raised their hands in volunteering to change the baby as often as possible: colostrum has a laxative effect, helping your baby pass those early stools, which aids in the excretion of excess bilirubin and helps prevent jaundice (that yellow color in newborns that makes them look like a character on the Simpsons).

My Advice? Please purchase many, many diapers very early in the pregnancy.

Now noticing your wife's new and improved breasts, you will want to touch them all of the time. "No!" "No!" "No"! she says. "Those are for the baaaaaaby!" And this is why lions eat their cubs.

This can be a nightmare for some men. It's like seeing that Maserati behind glass doors under lock and key. You can see it just fine, but you can't get close to it. And all you want to do is touch it, sniff it, frolic in its exquisite essence.

My Advice? This is a tough one (man-to-man) as I don't usually tell men to stay away from your wife's breasts. So all I can say is, "Deal with it." The sad truth is, you are now second banana. And it's not only her breasts that are involved here. It's pretty much everything else as well. Her time. Her money. Your money. Her affections. I know it's hard, but you are just going to have to sit back and visually enjoy them from afar. Right now, that's about all you got. Remember: "Respect the breast."

Okay, you can invite the woman back in.

Now that you have rejoined us, I would like to say that, yes, I was being a little sexist for a bit. But the truth is, all men, yes even your sweet baboo, are pigs. That's something you will have the rest of your life to contemplate. One additional thing you both need to be aware of is the so-called Madonna Complex.

Author's Note: Technically, its formal name is The Madonna/Whore Complex. I am a little (a lot) squeamish about that term. I find it a bit unsettling. So for our purposes, I will simply refer to it as The Madonna Complex. If you need to be angry about this, you can literally blame it all on Sigmund Freud.

Rather than get too pedantic about this whole mess, it's a guy thing. And allegedly it goes back to unresolved mommy issues that I really don't want to get into in a big way. However, it's important enough to note that after your child is born, the male usually will exhibit signs of it.

Everybody just relax. It will pass.

REAL ADVICE

Without going back to how the complex may have manifested itself in your courtship days, it's after the child is born is where we will start.

While there is really no set time when to resume having sex again, most MD's advise at least three weeks. That might be cutting it a bit close. Remember the woman has just passed the equivalent of a bowling ball between her legs, and she is a bit sore and very, very tired. Have some sense about when to "restart" all the frolicking. Fact is, once everything gets back to normal body-wise and the woman is able to fit back into her "normal" clothes, and is not way too tired from those 3am feedings, everything (including sex) can get back to normal. This can take up to six weeks or longer.

Or does it?

Stay with me here. It is at this point that if the Madonna Complex has not been evidenced before, it can (sometimes) come into play. You see, all of a sudden, to the husband, the wife is no longer just a wife (or even just a woman for that matter). She is now the mother of a child. And as such, a man may begin to think of his wife as a mother and not an appropriate sexual partner.

Author's Note: This is mostly for the women. When you are ready to begin sexual relations with your husband at a suitable point, but your husband is a tad reluctant, it's not because, "What, you don't find me attractive anymore?" "I don't look good to you?" "What, I smell like dirty diapers? "There's someone else, isn't there?

No. No. No. And no. What the wife might be misconstruing for ostracism is that whole Madonna Complex scenario.

All along the husband has been having sex with a sexual, unattached (except for the marriage thing) woman. She is no longer that. She is a mother like his mother, and sex with mom is well, sick. "You are a mom. My mom was a mom. One doesn't have sex with one's mother in polite society. Hell, I didn't even want my dad to have sex with her."

As stupid to some of you who are reading this sounds, let me reassure you: it is very real. Google it.

My Advice? This is one of those, "We need to sit down and talk about this" moments. The wife truly needs to feel secure concerning all of this, and it's only fair. Everyone has to remember that she physically had a child. Now, she's undoubtedly doing so much more, and she has every right to attend to her motherly duties including facing the smells and stains that come along with it. So, husbands, assure her that her worries about her physical attractiveness are not correct. It is more of an emotion problem you are dealing with at the moment. Be honest about this phase of your relationship. And it is a phase. Be patient about this as well. Everything will resolve itself given enough honesty and time.

Whew! We all got through that part with pretty much everything intact. So on to the next.

There exists a worldwide billion-dollar industry related to child rearing and everything that goes along with it. Books, blogs, magazines, seminars, and on and on and on exist to tell you how to properly raise your little one so that he/she doesn't end up on some psychoanalyst's couch telling him or her what assholes the parents were. This is not one of them books. That would take much too long and create way too many words. Plus, far be it for me to give you all my thoughts on this portion of your married life. It's much too complicated.

So, to help things along, I'm going to now give you things to consider before and after any child rearing is to be done. In other words, I'll make the list so you don't have to find a pencil in that junk drawer.

My Advice?

Find New Friends: This is not to say that many of your friends are not cool. They may very well be, and you don't have to let go of them completely. Unfortunately, your visits to your single and/or childless friends will become less frequent. It just naturally happens. You will need and want to spend more time with friends that are plotting the same course as you. Watch them. Learn from them. Then don't do what they do.

Make Amends With Those In-laws: Family support systems, as messy and fraught with danger as they can often times be, are crucial, if not essential to help you in the later part of your pregnancies and the early stages of child rearing. Here's when the Colonel and Martha come in handy. But be advised, Martha may want to fill you up with all her child rearing advice and abilities. She may question your every move. If so, give her a job(s) to do such as cleaning up the baby's crib area, folding the baby's laundry, or tidying up the baby's dresser. Notice that these jobs serve the baby's universe, which will make her happy, but doesn't involve actually touching the baby, which makes you happy.

Grow Up: Sorry. Didn't mean to be so blunt, but the truth is, you are steadily on your way to becoming your parents, and we can't have that interfered with, can we? There aren't many more nights with your asshole friends down at Clancy's. Not many more wine and cheese tasting get-togethers. Not many more book club readings to attend. There's not much more of anything except taking care of junior/angel. If you need (or think you need) to go to France, or save a whale, or cure leprosy, do it before the baby comes. As a case in point, there has never been a scientist with a husband/wife at home with the baby who has ever cured cancer. Think about it.

Money, Money, Money: It should go without saying that you need to get your finances in order before you even think about having a child. But, you evidently bought this book because you had some lingering doubts as to your abilities. So, let me say it thusly: Get your finances in order before you even think about having a child. Remember what I said much earlier in this book: It can cost upwards to $295,000 to raise a child up to the age of 18. By the way, among all the other things you will need to stock up on, you're gonna need a new car. A much bigger one.

Agree On Your Respective Parenting Philosophies: Again, it should go without saying, but do this before you have a child. Go to a local day care center once or twice a week. Have some of the little ones sit on your lap who are waiting to go to the bathroom. Go to the zoo and agitate the monkeys who will then fling their feces at you. Go to the loudest punk band bar you can find, and without drinking anything, stay for an hour. In short, enter the fifth circle (anger) of Dante's Inferno. Have fun with that.

Resolve Any Leftover Conflicts: This is sort of two-fold. First, if you two haven't been getting along (I know all couples fight every now and again), resolve the issues. And I cannot stress this enough: A new baby will not, I repeat, will not solve your marital problems. Trust me on this.

REAL ADVICE

Secondly, if either one of you has any unresolved issues/problems from childhood (like that Madonna thing), reconcile it (them). No good taking care of someone else if you are still carrying baggage from unresolved "growing up" issues.

Speaking of conflicts, you two are going to fight about babies. You two are going to compromise about babies. You two are going to cry about babies. And you two are going to figure it all out. Millions of folks who came before you have had many happy successes with starting a family. I have faith that you two will also.

That's it. We're done here. If you have stayed this long, there's only one chapter to go. I know, and frankly, I'm pretty excited about it to.

CHAPTER TEN

What Have We Learned Here Today?

Well, we've successfully navigated through all the things in your life that initially attracted you two together, the first fights, the financials, the in-laws, the chores and birthin' babies. Maybe you learned a lot, maybe you didn't. But if this book got you both to thinking about some important things that are happening or going to happen in your life, then it has succeeded.

And that's the point. No one book or seminar or blog or magazine or deluge of advice from friends and family is going to steer either one of you to all of the right answers. Life and relationships just don't work that way. They can only work the way you (and now, your spouse) want them to work. And even then, only maybe.

Being a good and faithful advice giver, I'm going to help this problem along. Now we both know how much I hate lists, but I'm assuming you still can't find anything in your junk drawer to write with, so I'm going to give you a list of things that may aid you in your marital endeavors.

REAL ADVICE

I struggled a bit with all of this because hierarchies, no matter how well researched, are always speculative. So if you think number six seems a bit too high or low on the list, well, too bad. Change the order of things on your own. Good luck with that.

By the way, it is a Top Ten list. Do you know why almost everybody's lists are "Top Ten?" Well, my little newbies, it's because 10 is about most peoples level regarding memories. This is why telephone numbers contain the three-digit area code and the seven-digit phone number. That's about the most numbers strung together we can effectively remember without too much strain.

Communication

This doesn't mean you have to talk about every little thing that pops up in your life. This can make everyday life a bit mundane as well as boring. Also, remember that men communicate quite differently. The male is usually abrupt and communicates to transfer information. The female usually communicates on a more humanistic level and her communications is a bit more circuitous and transfers feeling as well as information. Don't remember whether I said it before (and I am not going to reread this book one more time), but for women: 20,000 words per day. For men: 7,000 words per day. There is no value judgment on this, and it obviously doesn't hold true for every man and woman. But on average, women speak almost three times as much as many men do every day.

The point is, regardless of the situation, any situation, don't ever stop communicating. Virtually everything that happens throughout your married life affects you both, and if there ever comes a time when splitsville is looming like an Oklahoma rain storm, you will probably be able to trace it back to: "I guess it all started when we just stopped talking to each other." Besides what man or woman wants to go through life on a steady diet of: "I thought you..." "I just assumed you..." "Didn't I tell you...?"

That's no way to live.

Trust

This is one that is so important. And, it should go without saying. But not everyone got that checkmark in that "Plays well and gets along with others." box on the kindergarten report card. Breaking a trust even if it is accidental, can lead to so much negative energy as well as reprisals. If you break a trust and your spouse finds out about it, you are going to experience those "Trust Issues" you are afraid your child will be telling his or her shrink someday. Trust me (no pun intended), losing trust in your partner can kill a marriage dead. So when in doubt, reread your wedding vows. Don't break 'em.

Handle Differences Creatively and As Partners

You cannot, will not, never will be able to do this unless you abide by numbers one and two. Ya gotta talk it out. Ya gotta have each other's backs. You did not marry your best friend. Sorry if this comes as a surprise to you. But you didn't. Your best friends on their best days can't ever hurt you as much as your spouse. Your best friends just can't make you feel as whole or as loved as your spouse can. The emotions you feel for your spouse, can never be compared to the emotions you feel for your best friend.

REAL ADVICE

If your best friend left you now, never to be seen again, yes, you would feel a pretty big loss. But if your spouse left you, never to be seen again? Well, hopefully you get the point.

You and your spouse are partners—and so much more. He or she represents everything, the entire culmination of your lives. The epitome of everything you hoped for and something you have yearned for pretty much all of your life.

But you will clash. You will fight. You will have differences of opinion. Hell, you two will see, or hear, or experience the same exact thing and interpret it completely different. That's okay. Just know that sometimes differences can't be resolved or resolved in a normal way. So they may need to be taken care of creatively. If your differences are not handled well enough, like my grandma asked, " Would you rather break up over something small or something big?" This is a rhetorical question, by the way. You needn't answer it. But a proper answer would be, "Neither." You don't want to break up at all.

Case in point is the old, "We don't spend enough time together," complaint. Well, of course you don't. You're probably both working eight to ten hours a day, and you're both so tired at the end of it, that you both pretty much don't spend enough time together. What to do? What to do? Be creative. Well, as creative as you can. I mean, one way to solve this is for one of you to quit working, while the other one cuts back to part time. Um, nope. The taxman, and the electric man, and the cable man won't like that solution at all. But, you can try and set a specific time during the workday to at least telephone each other and talk with one another without being intrusive. It won't always work, but it's certainly worth a try. And, it's at least something. Or, if you are both off on a Saturday and/or

Sunday and are not totally under the thumb of "The Man," forget the dishes, forget the lawn, and forget everything except for each other. It doesn't have to be an all day thing, but again, at least it's something, and you both may be better for it.

The point is sometimes we all have to be creative to make things work properly. Just always remember that you are partners. Solve your differences together as partners.

Erect Your Own Force Field

Truth be told, as newlyweds or about to be newlyweds, you two are simply going to have to establish boundaries against all comers: friends, friends of friends, in-laws, relatives, and so on. You both need to begin establishing your own routines and traditions centered around your marriage. You let those who you want to join in with you, join in. The others? Sorry, after you get married, you will begin to notice that you don't see Dave as much as you used to. You don't see Katie as much as you used to. Mark? Well, you don't even see him at all.

This is a fact of married life. Some friends stay, some don't. But you two decide. You two decide who will venture into your lives on a regular or semi-regular basis. Marriage means you lose some folks while picking up some new ones. This is the nature of the beast. You both need time to adjust to married life and begin a brand new path in order to be successful. Don't be shy or fret about this. You will, at some point, come to terms and make the necessary adjustments with it all. I believe in you, Bubbala.

REAL ADVICE

Agree On Money/Career Decisions

Sorry, but you are not always going to agree on these matters, but it's not worth getting hit over the head by a flying frying pan. Financial fights and disagreements over career choices (or lack of them) can be the worst and lead to all kinds of bad Karma. So will unemployment. If not handled properly, one of you is going to be sitting on the curb at the Gas and Gulp, sucking on a bottle of Wild Turkey, while the other drives slowly past you and waves goodbye to you. We don't want that now do we?

Regarding all of the financial problems you two will experience, I wish I could give you some really cool advice on how to either avoid them altogether, or solve them when they pop up. But the reality is that financial/career problems are like the Whack-A-Mole. Sometimes it takes constant pounding, along with a whole lot of misses to deal with them effectively. And even then, sometimes you take home the little Kewpie Doll, sometimes that big stuffed bear.

What I'm trying to say here is that both of you need to keep clear heads and try, really try to be as objective and unemotional about these matters as possible. And here is where you are really going to need to find that damned pencil in your junk drawer. Work it out, and work it out as a team. You must be supportive of one another or all you will get is, "You are nothing but a dream crusher!" Notice I actually ended that last sentence with an exclamation point. I hate exclamation points, but it represents rising voices and tempers.

When I worked at the advertising agency many years ago, we used to have many meetings on where we wanted to take the clients' products or services. In order to do so, we had a lot of meetings. A lot.

Everyone came to these meetings with all sorts of ideas and plans and very large and healthy egos. It was important that no ones spirits were crushed in the whole process. These meetings were always held using deferred judgment (and a whole lot of Post-it notes). That simply meant that any idea was noted and never dismissed out of hand. Every idea was written on a note and attached to the wall. After everyone who wanted to contribute was exhausted, we would take the notes, one by one and remove those that were either not possible or unworkable. This was a variation on the Aristotelian Dialectic Method for finding absolute truth (Think also, Occam's Razor). And it takes forever. But...the last note still stuck to the wall was the closest thing to the absolute truth there was, and so we went with it, usually with pretty good results.

The point is, you two need to find your own absolute truths about finances. Only you can understand the thoughts and logic that you are able to apply. Go with that last note on the wall. That's probably your answer. It may take awhile, but at least you two will find agreement.

Commitment, Patience, Forgiveness

I know, this is sort of one of those catchall sections where stuff goes when you can't think of any other place to put it. And, it's one of those categories that should go without having to say it. But because we are all human, you really can't be surprised that most folks forget their commitments to you. Most folks lose their patience with you. Most folks at some time or another just won't go down the forgiveness trail. And even though you are not most folks, think back to when you forgot a promise or two; when you lost your patience with someone; when you found it hard to forgive.

Trust me, we all lose our way. We don't always keep our promises. We don't always have patience with every little thing life throws at us (usually at about 90 miles per hour), and we sure as hell don't forgive all those crummy slights we get on a day-to-day basis. And for the 50th time: It's because we are all human, and therefore fallible.

Through everything that you two will go through, just remember that you both made a commitment to be committed. You both promised to be patient with each other. You both promised to forgive each other's shortcomings. Always, always, always, even in the darkest hours, remember that marriage is not life's version of The Hokey-Pokey. You can't operate your relationship by putting one foot in and one foot out. "Both hands and feet inside the window, please." Marriage is more like Twister, where you are both tangled up with each other, and sometimes you have to stretch really hard to make it all work. So be bendy (think willow tree).

If you are ever having problems with these three things (Commitment, Patience, Forgiveness), get out one of those post-it notes you used for the financial/career section and write the words backwards on it. Then, staple it to your forehead if you have to. And each time you forget one or all three of these things, go to the mirror in your bathroom and read them. Now repeat after me: "Dumb ass." That should do it.

Do Your Part

This doesn't mean just do what you promised to do. It means not everybody is able to do all of the things they promised to do. Life keeps getting in the way. I know, one of you promised to do such and such around the house on a daily/weekly/monthly basis. But man, try and keep up with just the original stuff you promised to do. As you go through your married life, there are always additions to your lives that need to be handled, either as a couple or individually. This is hard work.

So when your spouse comes home, and he or she is confused, tired, constipated, or just sick of all the crap that happened that day—Do Your Part. Do it. Just go ahead and do it. Do it. For God's sake, even if you have never done it before, do it now. Take out the garbage, vacuum, cook dinner, change the damn light bulb. Whatever. Your part is not what you promised you would do as far as helping around the house or helping out with finances, or helping out in dealing with "The Man" on your spouse's behalf. Your part is to make your spouse more comfy and safe in times of troubles. It's that simple.

Empathy

Allegedly, your marriage to each other was a union, whereby you were joined as one. Easy to use it as a slogan for your coffee cup, but really, really hard to do on a daily basis.

And in case you are not sure about the exact definition of the word empathy, it can be described as an emotion whereby you not only sense others' emotions, but you also have the ability to imagine clearly what the other person is feeling. There are a whole bunch of warm and fuzzy synonyms associated with it, but the big three are: appreciation, insight, and sympathy.

REAL ADVICE

Everyone (sinner or saint, rich or poor, single or married) is just trying to accomplish one thing as they go about their way in life: getting through their day without getting yelled at, at least not too much.

But that's not often the case. Many days (as we all know), that doesn't happen. And so you come home after taking your portion of misery and problems for eight to ten hours, only to find that your spouse experienced the same thing.

It's not a question of who goes first in laying out the litany of problems they have had during their day, it's a question of who is able to listen and not only sympathize, but show empathy as well.

A pretty famous case concerning empathy was during an oil crisis many years ago. Short on gas and oil, Americans were advised to turn their heater down to 68 degrees during cold weather. To show that this was a group effort, everybody from the president on down appeared on TV wearing a sweater. The idea here was to let everyone know that they were in this with you. Maybe you also remember President Clinton's famous, "I feel your pain." Trite? Maybe. Effective? Absolutely.

Be Clinton.

Romance And Sex

Regarding sex and romance (or romance and sex), show up, but don't just show up. Stay in relatively decent shape. Don't wear crappy clothes all the time (especially to bed). Shave. Fix your hair (both of you). And for God's sakes, take a shower.

In short, keep finding ways. Have romance. Have sex. Google it if you have to, but have sex.

We're done here.

Show Up

I've said it, you've heard it, but it bears repeating. Ninety percent of a successful marriage requires you to pretty much just show up. There is a whole hell of a lot crammed into the other 10%, but hopefully you've learned something from reading this book.

Always be there for her. Always be there for him. And when in doubt if you two are going through some rough waters, refer back to the Commitment, Patience and Forgiveness section. You made those promises. You would take a bullet for your spouse. You would throw yourself under the bus for him. For her. Those promises are easy to make when there's no hint of conflict. Much, much harder when that big bus is coming right at your beloved. It's what you do in that next moment that will define your marriage, as well as your commitment.

Marriage is a wonderful, beautiful experience. And chances are that both of you will experience the utmost joy and pleasure derived from one another. There will be many, many times when your mutual love and joy for and with each other will be so intense that you think the top of your head will blow off.

But also know, that you can't get to that point without putting in the work. And it is sometimes hard. But you have to show up and do your part; for yourself; for each other.

REAL ADVICE

That about does it. Once again, congratulations on the nuptials. Live long, live happily, live strong.

Let me leave you with this short poem by an unknown author:

> When the one whose hand you're holding
>
> Is the one who holds your heart
>
> When the one whose eyes you gaze into
>
> Gives your hopes and dreams their start,
>
> When the one you think of first and last
>
> Is the one who holds you tight,
>
> And the things you plan together
>
> Make the whole world seem just right,
>
> When the one whom you believe in
>
> Puts their faith and trust in you,
>
> You've found the one and only love
>
> You'll share your whole life through.

Acknowledgments

This page is dedicated to those people and institutions that have been instrumental in bringing this project to life. In no particular order, they include:

Relentlessly Creative Books: who took a chance on an unknown.

Monica Rix Paxson: Publisher at Relentlessly Creative Books. Her unwavering faith and dedicated efforts on my behalf have truly been remarkable.

Thomas Maher: My one and true friend, who never asked "Why? but "Why not?"

Rene Pietroburgo: Just her smile and trust in me has been enough.

Siggy Buckley: A gifted author in her own right. She's always been there for me, through all those thin times. Can't thank her enough.

Matthew Pietroburgo: Tech Wizard and Maze Guide. And not one complaint.

Mark Waters: One of the most giving men I have ever met. Thank you, my brother.

Judy Fox: Because she's just, well, Judy.

All my friends: All those of you that have put up with my ever-changing moods and ever-present anxieties while projects such as this preoccupied my time and my energies. Thank you for your loyalty and patience.

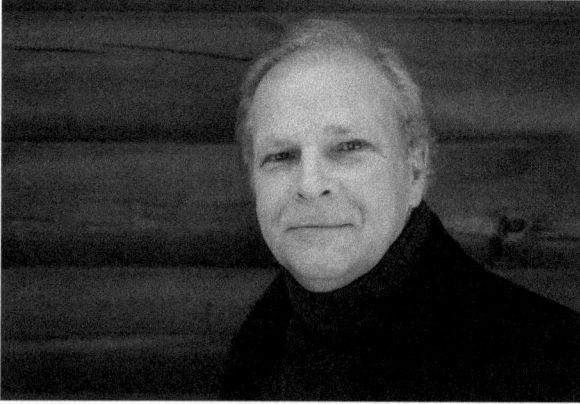

ABOUT THE AUTHOR

Best-selling author, editor and raconteur, Samuel Murphy, former educator and CEO of The William Murphy Advertising Agency, spent several years researching family and marital relationships, child rearing, unemployment and personal finances. Much of the data from his research resulted in the publishing of his first book, *Real Advice for the Unemployed* and the second in the series, *Real Advice for the Newlywed.*

Murphy's frank and friendly style, perfected in many articles and short stories involving the poignant and personal side of life that revolves around the impact of personal choices and significant changes in peoples' lives—especially when those choices are made during stressful times.

Mr. Murphy lives in a log home that he constructed on the Gulf of Mexico side of Florida with his wife, children and many animals.

To learn more, please visit http://murphysrealadvice.com/

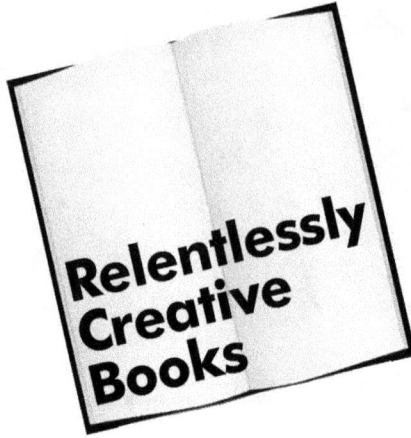

About the Publisher

Relentlessly Creative Books™ offers an exciting new publishing option for authors. Our "middle path publishing™" approach includes many of the advantages of both traditional publishing and self-publishing without the drawbacks. For more information and a complete online catalog of our books—

Please visit us at
RelentlesslyCreativeBooks.com

or write us at
books@relentlesslycreative.com.

For readers, join our online Readers Group and enjoy free eBooks, sneak previews on new releases, book sales, author interviews, book reviews, reader surveys and online events with Authors. Register at RelentlesslyCreativeBooks.com.

www.ingramcontent.com/pod-product-compliance
Lightning Source LLC
Chambersburg PA
CBHW051956090426
42741CB00008B/1415